Vegetation Classification of Mount Rainier, North Cascades, and Olympic National Parks

Plant Association Descriptions and Identification Keys

Natural Resource Technical Report NPS/NCCN/NRTR—2009/211

Rex C. Crawford
Natural Heritage Program
Washington Department of Natural Resources
Olympia, Washington 98503-1749

Christopher B. Chappell
Independent Contractor
Santa Fe, New Mexico, 87507

Catharine C. Thompson
National Park Service
Olympic National Park
600 E Park Ave
Port Angeles, Washington 98362

F. Joseph Rocchio
Natural Heritage Program
Washington Department of Natural Resources
Olympia, Washington 98503-1749

April 2009

U.S. Department of the Interior
National Park Service
Natural Resource Program Center
Fort Collins, Colorado

The Natural Resource Publication series addresses natural resource topics that are of interest and applicability to a broad readership in the National Park Service and to others in the management of natural resources, including the scientific community, the public, and the NPS conservation and environmental constituencies. Manuscripts are peer-reviewed to ensure that the information is scientifically credible, technically accurate, appropriately written for the intended audience, and is designed and published in a professional manner.

Natural Resource Technical Reports are the designated medium for disseminating the peer-reviewed results of scientific studies in the physical, biological and social sciences for both the advancement of science and the achievement of the National Park Service's mission. The reports provide contributors with a forum for displaying comprehensive data that are often deleted from journal because of page limitations. Current examples of such reports include the results of research that addresses natural resource management issues; natural resource inventory and monitoring activities; resource assessment reports; scientific literature reviews; and peer reviewed proceedings of technical workshops, conferences, or symposia.

Views, statements, findings, conclusions, recommendations and data in this report are solely those of the author(s) and do not necessarily reflect views and policies of the U.S. Department of the Interior, NPS. Mention of trade names or commercial products does not constitute endorsement or recommendation for use by the National Park Service.

Printed copies of reports in these series may be produced in a limited quantity and they are only available as long as the supply lasts. This report is also available from the Natural Resource Publications Management website (http://www.nature.nps.gov/publications/NRPM) on the internet.

Please cite this publication as:

Crawford, R. C., C. B. Chappell, C. C. Thompson, and F. J. Rocchio. 2009. Vegetation classification of Mount Rainier, North Cascades, and Olympic National Parks. Natural Resource Technical Report NPS/NCCN/NRTR—2009/211. National Park Service, Fort Collins, Colorado.

NPS D-586, April 2009

Contents

Figures

Tables

Appendices

Appendix A. Key to and descriptions of the plant associations of the Mount Rainier, North Cascades including the Chelan National Recreation Area, and Olympic National Parks.

Appendix B. Preliminary key to wetland and riparian plant associations of the Mount Rainier, North Cascades including the Chelan National Recreation Area, and Olympic National Parks.

Appendix C. Synthesis Tables of plant associations sampled at Mount Rainier, North Cascades including the Chelan National Recreation Area, and Olympic.

Appendix D. Environmental variables of plant associations sampled at Mount Rainier, North Cascades including the Chelan National Recreation Area, and Olympic National Parks.

Appendix E. Legacy plot data evaluated at Mount Rainier, North Cascades including the Chelan National Recreation Area, and Olympic National Parks.

Appendix F. Literature cited in descriptions of plant associations of the Mount Rainier, North Cascades including the Chelan National Recreation Area, and Olympic National Parks.

Appendix G. Sampling instructions and field forms used at Mount Rainier, North Cascades including the Chelan National Recreation Area, and Olympic National Parks.

Executive Summary

The Mount Rainier (MORA), North Cascades (NOCA) and Olympic National Parks (OLYM) vegetation classification project was a collaborative effort between the NCCN and the Washington Natural Heritage Program (WNHP) to create a vegetation classification at the association level for these three large parks. The association level is the finest scale of the National Vegetation Classification System (NVC). The system is hierarchical and uses both structural characteristics and species composition to classify vegetation types.

The vegetation classification for these parks was developed to a great extent from existing national, regional and local vegetation classifications. Previous classification work incorporated into this study included: 1) the 2005 coastal forests correlation project (CFCP Meidinger et al. 2005), 2) the 2005 version of the NVC (FDGC 2008, NatureServe 2005) and 3) the WNHP state vegetation classification.

Vegetation plots used in re-enforcing, validating, and developing the classification units included legacy plots collected on the parks, and map assessment plots and plant classification inventory plots collected by NPS field crews between 2005 and 2007. Plot data collected during the course of the project were assigned to previously defined associations and plots not falling within the variation of existing types were used to define new classification units when appropriate

The final classification evaluated 3396 plots: 2479 legacy plots and 917 classification plots from NPS crews. Based on this classification, a total of 311 upland and forested wetland associations are described. Over half (188) of the described associations are tree-dominated, 53 are shrub-dominated, 43 are herbaceous-dominated and 27 are sparse vegetation types. Of those associations, forty-nine may occur in the parks based on description from literature in adjacent areas but are not represented by current plot data from within park boundaries. 50 herbaceous and shrub-dominated wetland types are classified separately.

The association descriptions include scientific name, common name, a NatureServe Code when present, acronym (that cross-references to synthesis tables), NVC hierarchy levels including alliance, classification confidence, range in Washington, environmental features, USFWS wetland classification, vegetation description, state conservation rank, rank justification, comments, and plant association synonyms in previous classifications.

Along with the association descriptions, a field key to plant association identification was also generated, with a separate key for the wetland types. Additional supporting information includes synthesis tables of constancy and cover values, and tabular environmental data.

The plant associations described in this report reflect the most current and comprehensive vegetation classification not only for the parks, but for the region. The field keys and descriptions which comprise this report create a new framework for measuring, monitoring and mapping vegetation in the NCCN.

Acknowledgements

This project was completed through the effort and dedication of many individuals and organizations.

Numerous individuals collected plot, observation point, and field data that were incorporated in the classification. We appreciate the hard work of the NPS 2005-2007 vegetation mapping project field crews, which included W. Arneson, J. Chenoweth, W. C. Clark, I. Cunningham, P. Del Zotto, A. Francis, D. Graham, R. Gwodz, M. Immen, S. Johnson, S. Koenig, L. Koepke, M. Lee, C. Meredith, C. Meston, T. Morrison, L. Moulton, A. Nabors, K. O'Neil, G. Pappas, A. Peterson, E. Pruiksma, J. Runge, J. Waite, D. Wallace-Senft and M. Whisman. The NCCN vegetation group S. Acker (OLYM), M. Bivin (NOCA), L. Kurth (MORA), R. Rochefort (NOCA), and L. Whiteaker (MORA) assisted with project oversight, logistics support and reviewing drafts of this report.

NPS Data manager J. Boetsch contributed immeasurably to data management, organization and quality. For the WNHP, database management support and development was skillfully performed by Jack McMillen, particularly preparing data in VPRO (MS Access database) for analysis. The patience and cooperation of both data managers is greatly appreciated.

To these and other contributors to the success of the project, we are grateful.

Funding for this project was provided by the NPS Vegetation Mapping Program and the NPS Fire Program.

Introduction

Vegetation Classification Project

The Mount Rainier (MORA), North Cascades (NOCA) and Olympic National Parks (OLYM) vegetation classification project was organized and coordinated by the North Coast Cascades Network (NCCN) Inventory and Monitoring Program between 2005 and 2008. The purpose of this project was to describe existing plant associations and their environs at MORA, NOCA and OLYM, and to provide this information in written, tabular, and digital formats for vegetation mapping, park resource managers, and others. The basic project components consist of a vegetation classification including descriptions, field key, and supporting synthesis tables of plant associations.

A major purpose of the classification is to provide a platform for future National Park Service (NPS) vegetation mapping for all three parks. The final classification meets the national vegetation standards to the association level and documents the current organization of associations into alliance or other appropriate higher classification levels in anticipation of mapping at these higher levels. In 2005, the NCCN launched a multi-year project to complete vegetation classifications network park units. Project work was coordinated with the USGS-NPS Vegetation Mapping Program and NatureServe. Vegetation plot and observation point data collection occurred between 2005 and 2007. This report documents the methods, results and discussion of the NCCN vegetation classification project.

National Vegetation Classification Standard

This project utilizes the Federal Geographic Data Committee (FGDC 1997, FDGC 2008) - adopted National Vegetation Classification (NVC) standard. The NVC evolved from work conducted primarily by The Nature Conservancy (TNC), NatureServe, and the Natural Heritage Program network over more than two decades (Grossman et al. 1998). The structure of the NVC is based in part on an earlier international vegetation classification developed by the United Nations Educational, Cultural, and Scientific Organization (UNESCO 1973, Driscoll et al. 1984). Use of a standardized classification system helps to ensure data compatibility throughout the National Park Service and other agencies. The FGDC Vegetation Subcommittee continues to keep the NVC standard current and relevant. Substantial revisions to the upper levels of the NVC hierarchy were adopted by the FGDC in February 2008 (FDGC 2008).

Vegetation classification systems attempt to recognize and describe repeating assemblages of plants in similar habitats. The NVC (FGDC 1997) is a hierarchical system. The seven levels in the terrestrial vegetation classification are defined by both physiognomic characters and floristic criteria. The five upper levels (class, subclass, group, subgroup, and formation) are primarily based on physiognomic features. They have a broad geographic perspective and the floristic units have utility in local and site-specific applications (Grossman et al. 1998). Upper, physiognomic levels additionally contain physical, structural, and environmental characteristics identifiable from satellite imagery, aerial photography, or ground observations. In contrast to the upper levels, differences in floristic composition distinguish the two lowest levels of the 1997 NVC, alliance and association. The alliance and association levels form the base of the NVC hierarchy and are determined by the most abundant or diagnostic species comprising the various layers of a homogenous vegetation community. Species composition differentiates associations. An alliance is a physiognomically uniform group of associations sharing one or more diagnostic (dominant, differential, indicator, or character) species which, as a rule, are found in the uppermost stratum of the vegetation. (FDGC 1997). An association is defined as a plant community type with a consistent species composition, uniform physiognomy, and similar habitat conditions (Flahault and Schroter 1910).

The 2008 FGDC standard substantially revises the 1997 hierarchy. As stated in the 2008 standard (FGDC 2008):

> "The revised hierarchy addresses the following issues, among others: a) uses vegetation criteria to define all types (de-emphasizing abiotic criteria, such as hydrologic regimes in wetland types), b) provides a clear distinction between natural and cultural vegetation wherever these can be observed from broad growth form patterns (rather than combining natural and cultural vegetation initially and separating them at lower levels), c) for natural wherever these can be vegetation, defines the upper levels based on broad growth form patterns that reflect ecological relationships (rather than detailed structural criteria, which are more appropriate lower down in the hierarchy), d) provides a new set of middle-level natural units that bridge the large conceptual gap between alliance and formation, e) integrates the physiognomic and floristic hierarchy levels based on ecologic vegetation patterns, rather than developing the physiognomic and floristic levels independently and then forcing them into a hierarchy, f) provides detailed standards for plot data collection, type description and classification, data management and peer review of natural vegetation, and g) for cultural vegetation provides an independent set of levels that addresses the particular needs of cultural vegetation."

The 2008 natural vegetation hierarchy consists of eight levels, organized into three upper levels that include levels 1 through 5 in the 1997 standard, three middle levels not in the 1997 levels, and the same two lower levels as in the 1997. The FGDC 2008 standard fully discusses the rationale and criteria of each hierarchy level which are summarized in Table 1 (http://www.fgdc.gov/standards/projects/FGDC-standards-projects/vegetation/NVCS V2_FINAL_2008-02.pdf). In general, dominant growth form is more important in upper levels and diagnostic species and composition are more important in lower levels. The new middle level consider biogeographic and mesoclimatic factors along with diagnostic species and life forms.

Table 1. Criteria and rationale applied to each hierarchical level in the 2008 FGDC vegetation classification standard.

Hierarchy Level	Criteria
Upper:	**Physiognomy plays a predominant role.**
L1 – Formation Class Example – Mesomorphic Tree Vegetation	Broad combinations of general dominant growth forms that are adapted to basic temperature (energy budget), moisture, and substrate/aquatic conditions.
L2 - Formation Subclass Example –Temperate Forest	Combinations of general dominant and diagnostic growth forms that reflect global macroclimatic factors driven primarily by latitude and continental position, or that reflect overriding substrate/aquatic conditions.
L3 – Formation Example- Cool Temperate Forest	Combinations of dominant and diagnostic growth forms that reflect global macroclimatic factors as modified by altitude, seasonality of precipitation, substrates, and hydrologic conditions.
Middle:	**Floristics and physiognomy play predominant roles**
L4 – Division Example – Western North American Cool Temperate Forest	Combinations of dominant and diagnostic growth forms and a broad set of diagnostic plant species that reflect biogeographic differences in composition and continental differences in mesoclimate, geology, substrates, hydrology, and disturbance regimes.
L5 – Macrogroup Example - Vancouverian Lowland and Montane Rainforest	Combinations of moderate sets of diagnostic plant species and diagnostic growth forms, that reflect biogeographic differences in composition and sub-continental to regional differences in mesoclimate, geology, substrates, hydrology, and disturbance regimes.
L6 – Group Example - North Pacific Maritime Douglas-fir-Western Hemlock Forest	Combinations of relatively narrow sets of diagnostic plant species (including dominants and co-dominants), broadly similar composition, and diagnostic growth forms that reflect regional mesoclimate, geology, substrates, hydrology and disturbance regimes.
Lower:	**Floristics plays a predominant role**
L7 – Alliance	Diagnostic species, including some from the dominant growth form or layer, and moderately similar composition that reflect regional to subregional climate, substrates, hydrology, moisture/nutrient factors, and disturbance regimes.
L8 – Association	Diagnostic species, usually from multiple growth forms or layers, and more narrowly similar composition that reflect topo-edaphic climate, substrates, hydrology, and disturbance regimes.

The alliance and association levels of the revised hierarchy are essentially the same as the 1997 FGDC hierarchy. However, the distinctions between these two lower levels and the levels above have been clarified. The 2008 standard provides the following expanded definitions (FDGC 2008):

> **Alliance:** A vegetation classification unit of low rank (7th level) containing one or more associations, and defined by a characteristic range of species composition, habitat conditions, physiognomy, and diagnostic species, typically at least one of which is found in the uppermost or dominant stratum of the vegetation (Jennings et al. 2006). Alliances reflect regional to subregional climate, substrates, hydrology, moisture/nutrient factors, and disturbance regimes.

Association: A vegetation classification unit of low rank (8th level) defined on the basis of a characteristic range of species composition, diagnostic species occurrence, habitat conditions and physiognomy (Jennings et al. 2006). Associations reflect topo-edaphic climate, substrates, hydrology, and disturbance regimes.

NatureServe coordinates plant association data for the NPS vegetation mapping projects. Associations are added to the NVC and older concepts are refined as new data become available. Modifications to the NVC hierarchy are currently managed by NatureServe.

Project Overview

General Approach and Timeline

The vegetation classification for these parks was developed to a great extent from existing national, regional and local vegetation classifications. Plot data collected during the course of the project were assigned to previously defined associations and plots not falling within the variation of existing types were used to define new classification units when appropriate. Vegetation plots used in re-enforcing, validating, and developing the classification units included legacy plots collected on the parks, and map assessment plots and plant classification inventory plots collected by NPS field crews between 2005 and 2007. A preliminary classification was developed in 2005, and applied by field crews. NPS field data and legacy plot data were incorporated in 2006. NPS field crews directed efforts to fill known gaps in regional and local classifications and in legacy data during the 2006 and 2007 field seasons. The classification was modified following each field season and then used and verified by field crews in the following year. The overall sampling density is relatively limited considering the large areas encompassed by these parks, representing 1 plot per approximately 670 acres, although all major vegetation types were sampled. The final classification was completed in 2009.

Primary Partners and Project Roles

This project was a collaborative endeavor between the National Park Service, North Coast Cascades Network Inventory and Monitoring Program and the Washington Natural Heritage Program. NatureServe has also played a role. The NCCN staff generated the initial proposal for funding the three year project. NPS provided project oversight, field staff, developed a field data protocol and created and maintained the database used to store and manage plot data. The WNHP was selected as a partner for the classification analysis because of their extensive work to develop classifications of native plant communities throughout Washington State. WHNP staff has extensive experience in all phases of development of vegetation classifications and employs the same national system of classification used by the NPS. Thus, the project advances the objectives of both NPS and WNHP, and takes advantage of the strengths of both organizations. The WNHP was responsible for analyzing field data, updating the draft classification annually and preparing the final report. In 2008, NatureServe joined the effort and was primarily responsible for developing the upper levels of classification in the context of the new hierarchy.

Study Area

Location and Setting

Mount Rainier, North Cascades, and Olympic National Parks are located in western Washington. Regionally, these parks occur in the coastal ranges in the Pacific Northwest: the Cascade and Olympic Mountains. All three parks are primarily montane forest environments, however each park hosts unique features discussed in sections below. While occurring in the same broader setting, each park does contain unique characteristics due to differences in geological history, local climate, and past land use. These differences are reflected in the ecoregions in which each park resides (Figure 1).

Figure 1. Location of Mount Rainier (MORA), North Cascades Complex (NOCA), and Olympic National Parks with respect to the eight ecoregions of Washington State.

Mount Rainier National Park

Mount Rainier National Park (MORA), the nation's fifth national park, was established by an act of Congress in 1899 (NPS 2008a). MORA boundaries encompass 235,625 acres entirely west of the Cascade Range crest. The park is located in Pierce and Lewis counties, about 50 miles southeast of the Seattle-Tacoma metropolitan area (NPS 2008a; Figure 1). National Forest lands, including four wilderness areas, surround MORA to the north, east, and south while private lands occur to the west, much of which has been intensively logged (Biek 2000).

MORA is in the West Cascades ecoregion which, in Washington, includes the Cascade Mountains south of Snoqualmie Pass and west of the Pacific crest to the Oregon border (Figure 1) (WADNR 2007). The ecoregion extends southward to the Oregon-California border. Typical elevation range of the West Cascades is 500 to 7,000 feet with Mount Rainier (14,410 feet) as the high point and Columbia River Gorge (50 feet) as the lowest elevation. Mount Rainier, an active volcano that last erupted approximately 150 years ago, is the most prominent peak in the Cascade Range and dominates the landscape of a large part of western Washington State (NPS 2008a).

North Cascades National Park Service Complex

The U.S. Congress established North Cascades National Park Service Complex (NOCA) in 1968 to preserve "certain majestic mountain scenery, snowfields, glaciers, alpine meadows, lakes and other unique glaciated features" … "for the benefit, use and inspiration of present and future generations" (NPS 2008b). NOCA includes 684,237 acres of federally protected land near the crest of the Cascade Mountains from the Canadian border south to Lake Chelan (Figure 1). NOCA is approximately 62 miles (100 km) long and 31 miles (50 km) wide (Agee and Kertis 1987). NOCA was envisioned primarily as a wilderness park and 634,614 acres, or 93%, of the complex has been designated as the Stephen Mather Wilderness Area (NPS 2008b). NOCA is the core of over 2 million acres of federally designated wilderness in north-central Washington and is one of the largest such areas in the lower 48 states (NPS 2008b).

NOCA is in the North Cascades ecoregion which includes the Cascades Mountains north of Snoqualmie Pass and west of the Pacific Crest and extends into British Columbia (Figure 1). Most of the ecoregion lies between 1,000 and 7,000 feet elevation with the highest peaks rising to over 10,000 feet and valley bottoms at 500 feet (WADNR 2007). These mountains contain various metasedimentary rocks and display many glacially carved U-shaped valleys and cirques and a few volcanic peaks.

Olympic National Park

Olympic National Park (OLYM) was created in 1938 and covers 922,651 acres that span a rich and varied terrain. OLYM includes an outer coast strip comprised of rocky shorelines, beaches and coastal forests as well as one of the richest old-growth forests in the world (McNulty 2003). The Park is located on the Olympic Peninsula in northwestern Washington and is surrounded by Olympic National Forest and Washington Department of Natural Resource lands (Figure 1). OLYM is in the Northwest Coast ecoregion which includes the coast ranges from Oregon north to Vancouver Island, British Columbia (Figure 1). The Olympic Peninsula is bordered by the Pacific Ocean to the west, the Strait of Juan de Fuca to the north, and Hood Canal to the east while the southern flanks adjoin the lowlands of Grays Harbor basin (WADNR 2008).

Geology

The geologic history of each park shapes current vegetation patterns through its effects on topography, soils, and disturbance regimes. The following provides a brief geological history of the region and then specific geological processes related to vegetation patterns for each park.

Collision and accretion of terranes and volcanic activity at the leading contact of the North American plate underlie the geological history of the three national parks (Williams 2002). About 150 million years ago, the western edge of the North American continent, located approximately where Idaho, Oregon, and Washington meet today, began to collide with the easterly track of the Pacific plate resulting in the "docking" of new rocks to the North American continent (i.e. Superterrane I) and thereby extending the western edge of North America into eastern British Columbia and northeastern Washington (Williams 2002). About 50 million years ago, Superterrane II docked against the Superterrane I rocks extending the edge of the North American continent into most of contemporary British Columbia and northern Washington, including the area now occupied by NOCA (Williams 2002). Approximately 20-30 million years ago, as the San Juan de Fuca plate subducted under North America, ocean floor basalts and their overlying sediments began pushing up against the North American plate and were uplifted to form the Olympic Mountains (Williams 2002).

As the subduction of the Pacific oceanic plate continued under North America, a series of volcanic eruptions began creating the foundation of the Cascade Mountains around 40 to 17 million years ago. Around nine million years ago, uplift of this foundation along with renewed volcanic activity built and continues to build the contemporary Cascade Range (Williams 2002). Granitic rocks and welded fragmental volcanic rocks resistant to erosion now comprise many of the higher peaks in the South Cascades (Pringle 2008). The character series of stratovolcanoes, a large, steep volcano built up of alternating layers of lava and ash or cinders also called composite volcanos, currently found in the Cascade Range including Mount Rainier (the oldest in Washington), Mount St. Helens, and Mount Adams, emerged through and built atop the older volcanic Cascades. More northerly stratovolcanoes such as Mount Baker and Glacier Peak emerged through the older landscapes in the North Cascades (Williams 2002).

Erosive actions of gravity, wind and water erosion have steadily modified the mountains resulting in the steep topography of contemporary landscapes. Glaciation is a major modifier of landscapes and during the ice age the development and movement of ice and ice melt had great effects on the coastal and Cascade ranges. Alpine glaciers modified and continue modify the Cascades and the Olympic Mountains. The last maximum ice advanced 14,000 years ago during which the Canadian continental ice sheet covered the North Cascades and advanced to surround the Olympics on the east and north.

Mount Rainier National Park
Mount Rainier is a stratovolcano in the volcanic-arc that forms the Cascade Mountains. It is situated 15 miles east of the Cascade Crest where the range is 60 to 90 miles wide (Pringle 2008). At 14,410 feet, Mount Rainier is superimposed on the eroded foundation of the older volcanic, intrusive, and sedimentary rock of the Cascade Mountains (Pringle 2008). The pyroclastic cone of Mount Rainier began forming approximately one million years ago. About 700,000 years ago, eruptions of andesitic flows began rapidly building the mountain even higher. Relatively recent eruptions (between 6,600 and 5,700 years ago) have modified the morphology of the summit. In the last 10,000 years, Mount Rainier has been estimated to have erupted more than 40 times (Pringle 2008). Early settlers noted eruptions of the volcano between 1820 and 1894 (Pringle 2008). Such volcanic activity has a large impact on vegetation patterns as a result of direct disturbances and subsequent effects on soil development and drainage patterns as

documented at Mount Helens (Dale et al. 2005). For example, these eruptions have been the source of numerous mudflows (or lahars) which have flowed down the mountain's major river drainages. Since Pleistocene glaciations, more than 60 lahars are thought to have flooded these river valleys (Pringle 2008). These lahars typically destroy much of the vegetation within their path. Forest development soon initiates following these events. The lahars also restructure the geomorphology of the drainages and thus the template upon which valley bottom vegetation develops. Gigantic rock avalanches and other mass wasting events such as rock and talus slides are other geologic disturbances affecting vegetation patterns (WADNR 2008). These events can destroy existing vegetation and set the template for future vegetation development. Volcaniclastic deposits effect soil characteristics such as porosity and nutrients. In relation to these geologic events, vegetation patterns are correlated to soil drainage characteristics and time since the last.

Glaciation has had an important role in eroding the mountain and many of the contemporary river valleys at MORA (Pringle 2008; WADNR 2008). Mountain glaciations have occurred repeatedly over the last 120,000 years. Glacial action, glacial outwash, and alluvial landforms all have a significant effect on contemporary vegetation patterns (Franklin et al. 1988). The variety of geomorphic templates, soil textures, and resulting drainage patterns has a profound influence on the type of vegetation that develops in areas affected by past glaciations.

North Cascades National Park Service Complex
North Cascades National Park is embedded in the Cascade Range, a vast mountain chain that extends from northern California to British Columbia (WADNR 2008; Tabor and Haugerud 1999). The Cascade Mountains consist of an active volcanic arc superimposed upon Paleozoic to Tertiary age bedrock. From the Pliocene (5 to 2 million years ago) to the recent, uplift has created high topographic relief around the active volcanoes (WADNR 2008). The vertical distance from valley floor to the North Cascade peaks ranges between 4,000 to 6,000 feet making the North Cascades one of the steepest mountain ranges in the conterminous United States (Tabor and Haugerud 1999). A complex mix of volcanic arcs, deep ocean sediments, basaltic ocean floor, ancient continents, and submarine fans create the geologic foundation of the North Cascades (Tabor and Haugerud 1999; WADNR 2008). Subsequent uplift, erosion, metamorphosis, plutonic intrusion, additional uplift, and the formation of volcanic arc modified these pieces into the contemporary geologic mosaic that currently comprises the North Cascades (Tabor and Haugerud 1999). Two Quaternary stratovolcanoes, Mount Baker at 10,781 feet and the second most active volcano in Washington and Glacier Peak at 10,451 feet, rise above and dominate the volcanic arc which formed in the North Cascades (WADNR 2008). Both volcanoes are thought to be less than one million years old. Glaciations, landslides, and fluvial erosion have created the steep terrain, jagged peaks, and deep canyons currently found in the North Cascades (Tabor and Haugerud 1999). Past volcanism, uplift, and mass wasting have been both a destructive and creative force in the development of vegetation patterns in NOCA.

During the Holocene glaciations, the Cordilleran Ice Sheet flowed over most of the North Cascade range and greatly modified the North Cascade landscape. Today, the North Cascades has over 300 glaciers and contain the greatest concentration of alpine glaciers in the conterminous United States (over half of those found in the lower 48 states) (WADNR 2008;

NPS 2008b). Glacial landforms such as eroded valleys, till, glacial outwash, and alluvial landforms have a significant determinant of the type of vegetation.

Olympic National Park

The Olympic Mountains, within which Olympic National Park is mostly embedded, form the core of the Olympic Peninsula. The Olympic Mountains were formed from the uplift of sedimentary (e.g. sandstones, mudstones, and shales) and volcanic rocks which were deposited over millions of years on a seafloor off the continental shelf (McNulty 2003). During the middle to late Miocene (18-9 million years ago), as these sedimentary and volcanic rocks were carried by the Farallon plate toward the North American continent, some were uplifted instead of subducted underneath the North American plate (Alt and Hyndman 2001; WADNR 2008; McNulty 2003). This collision caused the uplifted sedimentary rocks to be forced underneath and behind the uplifted basalts on the eastward edge of the Farallon plate (Henderson et al. 1989; McNulty 2003). Those sedimentary rocks which were subducted were subject to metamorphism resulting in the formation of semischist, slate, and phyllite (McNulty 2003). The basalts were forced into their present day horseshoe-like distribution around the eastern edge of the Olympics.

Pleistocene glaciations, associated with both alpine and continental ice, dramatically eroded the Olympic Mountains into the jagged, steep topography characteristic of the contemporary landscape (McNulty 2003). Alpine glaciers tended to further erode drainages already begun by fluvial erosion resulting in a widening, straightening, and flattening of preexisting river valleys into characteristic U-shaped valleys. The headwaters of these glaciated valleys are often very steep and jagged. Continental ice sheets descended into western Washington numerous times during the Pleistocene (McNulty 2003). These ice advances wrapped around the northern and eastern base of the Olympic Mountains and, along with outwash streams flowing around the southern flank of the mountains effectively isolated the Olympics from nearby landforms. This isolation resulted in the Olympic Mountains serving as a refugium during the Ice Age for many species, especially plants (McNulty 2003; Buckingham et al. 1995). The northern and eastern lobes of the continental ice dammed many of the rivers draining off of the Olympic Mountains creating fjord-like lakes in the river valleys. As with the other two parks, uplift and glaciations have had dramatic effects on vegetation patterns in the OLYM. Unlike the other two parks, volcanism is not a part of OLYM geologic history.

A portion of the OLYM also occurs along the rocky coast of the Olympic Peninsula. During the Oligocene and early Miocene (50-18 million years ago), deposition of marine nearshore clastic sediments occurred around the periphery of the Olympic Peninsula (WADNR 2008). Erosion-resistant sandstones and conglomerates today form the characteristic islands, sea stacks, and headlands along the western coastline of the Olympic Peninsula (WADNR 2008; McNulty 2003).

Climate

Pacific Northwest climate is created by the interactions between seasonally varying weather and the region's mountain ranges (Climate Impact Group 2008). Winter rain and snow and summer drought characterize the temperate, maritime climate of the Pacific Northwest. High pressure systems which develop in the Pacific Ocean have a strong influence on the seasonal tracks of precipitation. Typically, two-thirds of the precipitation occurs between October and March when the Pacific high pressure system moves south allowing low pressure systems to approach from the Pacific Ocean on the dominant westerlies (Franklin and Dyrness 1998). During that time the Pacific storm track brings frequent rain in the lowlands and snow in the mountains. Mount Rainier and Mount Baker vie for the honor of receiving the most snow than anywhere else on earth. A high pressure area develops off the coast of Oregon and Washington and, when persistent, generally keeps the Pacific Northwest fairly dry during late spring into early fall.

Climate in the low elevations west of the Cascades is characterized by mild year-round temperatures, abundant winter rains, and dry summers. Average annual precipitation in most places west of the Cascades is more than 30 inches. The western slopes of the Olympic and Coast mountain ranges typically receive about 118 inches per year, with some locations on the Olympic Peninsula exceeding 200 inches per year. Average annual precipitation in the Cascades typically exceeds 100 inches or more.

The Cascade and Olympic mountains are barriers to eastward moving storms resulting in rainshadow development on the eastside of the mountains, sometimes significantly reducing precipitation. The Olympic rainshadow is the most dramatic with 119 inches average annual precipitation at Point Grenville on the Pacific Coast, over 200 inches/year at Mount Olympus 45 miles to the northeast and 17 inches/year at Sequim another 30 miles northeast in the rainshadow. Equally important are rainshadows at Mount Rainier, Mount Baker and in the North Cascades. Temperatures are also lower and the number of sunshine days is greater on the east side of the Cascade Crest

Mount Rainier National Park
Climate varies with elevation and local topography. At lower elevations (mostly below 3,000 feet) mild temperatures occur year round and rain is the major form of precipitation. Mean annual precipitation is near 59 inches while mean winter temperatures are near 32^0 F and mean summer temperatures 79^0 F (Franklin and Dyrness 1988). The highest amount of annual rainfall in MORA occurs in this elevation zone in the northwest part of the park (e.g. Carbon River valley) where 180-210 inches of rainfall produces rainforests similar to those found on the Olympic Peninsula (Biek 2000). Between 2,500 and 4,700 feet, climate is predominantly temperate and receives an annual precipitation of approximately 102 inches, considerably more precipitation than lower elevations, and much of which falls as snow, an average annual of approximately 28 feet (Franklin and Dyrness 1998). Another climatic characteristic of this elevation zone is the occasional rain-on-snow events which can occur during winter months. Mean annual summer temperatures are near 58^0 F and mean winter temperatures near 26^0 F. Over 4,000 feet elevation, cold temperatures and snowfall define the climatic regime of the subalpine. At the Paradise Ranger Station in MORA, summer temperatures average 52^0 F while winter temperatures 26^0 F. Mean annual precipitation at Paradise is 104 inches (Franklin and Dyrness 1988). Snow depths average more than 50 feet at Paradise (Biek 2000). In 1971-1972, the second highest world record for annual snowfall occurred at Paradise with an accumulation of 93 feet. This amount held the world record until 1999, when annual snowfall at Mount Baker surpassed it by a few inches (NOAA 2008). In the northeast portion of MORA, where Mount Rainier creates a rainshadow, the subalpine is slightly drier and colder version than other subalpine areas in the park. Cold winters, deep snowpack, and cool summers characterize these areas (Franklin and Dyrness 1988). The climate in these areas is more characteristic of high elevations in eastern Washington. Above the subalpine (usually above 6,000 feet) temperatures become extremely

cold and at the highest elevations, where year round cold temperatures predominate and snowfall exceeds snowmelt, glaciers and permanent ice have formed.

Special microclimates generated by local landforms and weather patterns also influence vegetation patterns (Biek 2000). For example, snow depth can be limited in alpine areas and ridgelines due to desiccating winds producing drier vegetation patterns that might otherwise be expected. Conversely, during summer months when precipitation is sparse, fog and clouds can be important sources of moisture for some forest types along high ridges (Biek 2000). Aspect also plays a strong role in the development of microclimates. Cold-air drainage off of snowfields or down into valleys has a large influence on local climate.

North Cascades National Park Service Complex

Climate in the North Cascade National Park Service Complex (NOCA) varies greatly between the western and eastern portion of the complex due to the barrier imposed by the North Cascade range on westerly storms. Average annual snowfall also varies with approximately 70 inches in western lowlands, 516 inches at high elevations west of the Cascade crest, to 123 inches at Stehekin on Lake Chelan (Douglas 1969). As mentioned above, the world record for annual snowfall was recently recorded at Mount Baker with over 93 feet of snowfall (NOAA 2008). Precipitation is seasonally distributed with the majority of the total annual precipitation falling between late fall and early spring.

Precipitation at low elevations mostly consists of rain, high elevations have significant snowpack for many months, and middle elevations have significant snowpack which fluctuates over the course of the winter due to rain-on-snow events (Iachetti et al. 2006). However, due to the width of the North Cascades, the rainshadow effect develops west of the Cascade crest in contrast to the southern Cascades where rainshadows are typically observed east of the Cascade crest (except rainshadow effects due to the much larger stratovolcanoes such as Mount Rainier). Temperatures also vary from west to east with colder winters and warmer summers occurring in the eastern portion of the NOCA (Agee and Kertis 1987). Local rainshadow effects, aspect, and cold-air drainage also create microclimates. For example, an average of 100 inches precipitation falls at Upper Baker Dam while only 35 inches accumulates on Desolation Peak on Ross Lake, 25 miles to the east.

Olympic National Park

The climate of Olympic National Park (OLYM) varies according to elevation and location on the peninsula. The Olympic Mountains create a very strong rainshadow resulting in drastic changes in precipitation within only 25 miles. Over 200 inches of annual precipitation falls on the west side of the Olympic crest while only 20 inches occurs in the northeast portion of the peninsula (e.g. near Sequim) due to an intense rainshadow effect (Henderson et al. 1989). This is one of the steepest precipitation gradients in the world with only 34 miles separating the wettest location in the continental United States from the driest location along the Pacific coast, north of southern California (Buckingham et al. 1995). As with the other two parks, the seasonal movement of high pressure systems produces a wet-dry climatic cycle. Starting in late fall and continuing through early spring, southwesterly storms bring wet, mild weather to OLYM (Henderson et al. 1989). As these storms hit the Olympic Mountains and begin to rise, the moisture laden airs begins to drop much of its moisture. By the time these storms pass over the mountains they have lost much of their moisture resulting in a dramatic drop in annual precipitation in the northeastern part of the Olympic Peninsula. The wettest areas of OLYM occur at the highest elevations and in the southwest corner of the Park while the driest areas occur in the northeast. About 93% of annual precipitation falls between September and May leaving the summer months relatively dry (Henderson et al. 1989).

Rain is the predominant form of precipitation below approximately 985 feet elevation. Coastal areas in OLYM have the mildest climate in the Pacific Northwest, meaning it has the least amount of variation in temperature and moisture than other areas (Franklin and Dyrness 1988). Along the coast, annual precipitation averages between 79-118 inches and frequent fog and low clouds occur during the relatively drier summer months (Franklin and Dyrness 1988). Rain and snow are predominant between 985 to 2460 feet and snow is the major form of precipitation at higher elevations (Buckingham et al. 1995). Snow depth can reach over 20 feet in subalpine meadows (Henderson et al. 1989)

Soils

Soil formation is controlled by five factors: climate, organisms, relief, parent material, and time (Jenny 1941). These factors are quite variable across the three parks resulting in a diversity of soil types with unique chemical and physical properties such as moisture and nutrient availability. Extensive mapping and classification has not been conducted by the Natural Resources and Conservation Service within the parks thus much of this discussion is limited to broad patterns observed in each park.

Five major Soil Orders can be identified as likely being the most common in the three parks (Soil Conservation Service 1994; Henderson et al. 1989). These include: (1) Spodosols which form in coarse-texture, acid, parent material, are subject to leaching, and are commonly found underneath forest vegetation. Except for drier areas (e.g. areas within rainshadows), conditions favorable for Spodosol development exist in most areas of the three parks (Henderson et al. 1989); (2) Inceptisols are immature soils which show a moderate degree of soil development but not enough to show equilibrium with the environment in which they are found. In other words, with more time they will develop into another Soil Order. Inceptisols are likely very common throughout the region; (3) Entisols are the youngest and least developed soils. Two major types are recognized: Orthents, which develop on colluvium such as recently eroded slopes, landslides, etc. and Fluvents, which are common in floodplains; (4) Histosols are organic soils formed when organic matter accumulation is greater than decomposition due to anaerobic condition. Histosol are found in bogs, fens, and along some streams; and (5) Andisols, which are soils developed in volcanic ejecta (Henderson et al. 1989). Another characteristic of high elevation soils is the development of cryptobiotic soil crusts which bind soils particles together thereby increasing soil stability, increasing infiltration, reducing erosion, and aiding vegetation establishment via an increase in available nutrients and water for plants (NPS 2005).

In addition to the general patterns just described, each of the matrix forest Groups (see Vegetation section below) exhibit some common soil features. The North Pacific Maritime Douglas-fir-Western Hemlock Forest Group generally has moderately deep soils (shallower on steep slopes) that are of medium acidity, well aggregated, sandy loam to clay loam in texture, moderate (e.g. Cascades) to high (Olympic Peninsula) organic matter, and forest floors or O horizons 3-6 inches deep (Franklin and Dyrness 1988). Soils in the North Pacific Mesic Western Hemlock-Silver Fir Forest Group are often exhibit podzolization, meaning Spodosols are quite common. Forest floor depths range from 1-3 inches and in northern Washington can reach up to 12 inches (Franklin and Dyrness 1988). Spodosols are also quite common in the North Pacific Mountain Hemlock-Silver Fir Forest and Tree Island Group but the degree of podzolization varies greatly. Forest floor depths range from 2-4 inches (Franklin and Dyrness 1988). Soils in the Northern Rocky Mountain Whitebark-Limber Pine Woodland Group are also mostly Spodosols but generally have thinner forest floor depths than those found in the North Pacific Mountain Hemlock-Silver Fir Forest and Tree Island Group (Franklin and Dyrness 1988).

Mount Rainier National Park
Hobson (1976; as cited in NPS 2005) developed a soils classification for MORA based on geological origin, topography, and drainage features. According to this classification, four major soil groups support forests at MORA: (1) Tephra soils are derived from pyroclastic deposits. These are common in the subalpine and alpine meadows as well as in forests throughout the park (Franklin et al. 1988). According to *Keys to Soil Taxonomy* these soils would be classified as Andisols (Soil Conservation Service 1994); (2) Colluvial soils consist of coarse, unconsolidated material from a variety of sources. These soils are typically found on slopes at all elevations, especially on steep slopes and south-facing aspects. Younger colluvial soils would most likely be classified as Orthents and older soils could vary in type such as Inceptisols or Spodosols (Soil Conservation Service 1994); (3) Alluvial soils form from fluvial deposition resulting from historic glacial floods and contemporary flooding regimes. Thus, alluvial soils are found along stream and river valleys and alluvial slopes and fans (NPS 2005). More recent alluvium would be classified as Fluvents while older deposition could vary depending on moisture regime and vegetation (Soil Conservation Service 1994); and (4) Mudflow soils are derived from lahars and consist of a mixture of tephra, alluvium, and colluvium (NPS 2005). Many forest soils are classified as Spodosols. Histosols are found in bogs and fens and possibly along some streams at high elevations (Franklin et al. 1988). Many areas in the subalpine and alpine consist of bare rock and talus slopes with no soil development. Heavy recreation use in many subalpine meadows is resulting in the destruction of the cryptobiotic soil crust resulting in increased bare ground and erosion in many of these areas (NPS 2005).

North Cascades National Park Service Complex
The Natural Resources Conservation Service is currently mapping soils in NOCA (Toby Rogers, NRCS, personal communication 2009). Andisols and Spodosols are major soils and are associated with older soils. Andisols are formed from volcanic ash and posses what are called andic properties (high water-holding capacity and ability to fix and make unavailable to plants, phosphorous.) Younger soils, such as Inceptisols and Entisols, are typically associated with recently eroded slopes, riparian environments, landslides, etc. and are less influenced by volcanic ash since the origin these soils post-date past volcanic eruptions which deposited appreciable amounts of ash. As with much of the montane forest of western Washington, Spodosols are likely a common soil type underneath forests, Histosols are to be found in bogs and fens, Entisols are expected in areas recently exposed to erosion (Orthents) or deposition (Fluvents), Inceptisols are likely common in many forests, and Andisols may be associated with past volcanic eruptions.

Olympic National Park

Soil patterns for OLYM are briefly described here. More detailed discussion can be obtained in Henderson et al. (1989). As with the other two parks, soils have not been explicitly classified or mapped for OLYM. Complex geology, glacial history, range of precipitation, and a variety of relief have resulted in a rich diversity of soil types with many of the same general patterns described above for MORA (Henderson et al. 1989; NPS 2005). Spodosols and Inceptisols are common Soil Orders underneath forest within OLYM. Most Inceptisols on the Olympic Peninsula are likely developing toward Spodosols (Henderson et al. 1989). Orthents are common on colluvium and Fluvents are a common soil type along floodplains. Histosols are found in bogs and fens. Andisols are likely found in the OLYM as well but their extent is less clear (Henderson et al. 1989).

Hydrology and Water Resources

The variety of water resources found in each park is briefly described below.

Mount Rainier National Park

Approximately 400 lakes, 470 streams, several mineral and thermal springs, and about 3,000 acres of wetlands have been mapped at MORA (NPS 2008a). These aquatic resources support a diversity of plant and animal species and are critical habitat for several native amphibian and fish species, eight which are listed as endangered, threatened, or species of concern (NPS 2008a). In addition, other wildlife species are dependent on these aquatic ecosystems for a portion of their life cycle. Of the nine major rivers and their tributaries in the park, the Nisqually, Puyallup, Mowich, Carbon, West Fork, White, and Muddy Fork rivers are supported by seasonal precipitation and the mountain's 26 major glaciers (covering 35 square miles). The Ohanapecosh and Huckleberry drainages do not originated with glacial melt-water. All the park's rivers flow into Puget Sound near Tacoma, Washington except the Muddy Fork and Ohanapecosh Rivers that flow into the Cowlitz River and eventually into the Columbia River (NPS 2008a). Hot springs are found at Ohanapecosh and on mountain slopes near Paradise and Winthrop glaciers, a thermal lake is found in the firn caves on Mount Rainier's summit crater, and a mineral spring at Longmire (NPS 2008a). The ecological characteristics of these unique water resources remain relatively unknown. Various wetlands such as bogs, fens, marshes, wet meadows, aquatic beds, and riparian forests and shrublands are found throughout the park. Although they occupy a very small portion of the landscape, wetlands often support a disproportionately high percentage of landscape biodiversity (Flinn et al. 2008; Van Dyke 2008; Apostol and Sinclair 2006).

North Cascades National Park Service Complex

NOCA has a diverse array of water resources including over 500 lakes and ponds scattered throughout the landscape. Many of these are tarns, which are remnants of the alpine glaciers. Many of the lakes and ponds are surrounded by marshes and wet meadows (NPS 2008b). As at MORA, wetlands such as bogs, fens, marshes, wet meadows, and riparian wetlands provide important habitat and support a significant number of species. An impressive complex of wetlands (one of the largest in NOCA) occurs along the lower reaches of the Chilliwack River (NPS 2008b).

Five major rivers drain the NOCA landscape. The Chilliwack River flow originates in the northwest portion of the park and flows north into British Columbia's Fraser River, which is the largest watershed along the west coast of North America (NPS 2008b). The Nooksack River also originates in the northwest portion of the park and carries drainage from the north flanks of Mount Baker and Mount Shuksan (the only part of this watershed within NOCA) westward to the Puget Sound. The Baker River drains the Picket Range and the southeast slopes of Mount Baker and then flows into the Skagit River which continues westward through the middle of NOCA before flowing into Puget Sound (NPS 2008b). The Skagit River watershed, which originates in British Columbia, is the largest drainage emptying into the Puget Sound (NPS 2008b). The reach above the confluence with the Baker River drains a significant portion of the northeastern and middle sections of NOCA. Three hydroelectric dams, Gorge, Diablo and Ross, were built in the early 20th century along the Skagit River (2008b). The Stehekin River drains the southeast section of NOCA and flows into Lake Chelan, a glacially carved, long, deep (third deepest in the United States) lake. Lake Chelan's outlet drains into the Columbia River (NPS 2008b). Hundreds of small streams and headwater wetlands, which received melt-water from seasonal snowpack and glaciers, feed into all of these rivers.

Olympic National Park

Olympic National Park supports over 3,000 miles of rivers and streams, hundreds of lakes, a variety of wetland types, and 73 miles of coastline along Pacific Ocean (NPS 2008c). These habitats support a rich diversity of aquatic flora and fauna ranging from unique bog plants, endemic amphibians, salmon, to a diversity of marine life (McNulty 2003). A few large lakes occur within or border OLYM boundaries including Lake Crescent, Lake Ozette, Lake Quinault, and Lake Cushman. These lakes were created when deep troughs were carved by glaciers and remnant ice and melt-water filled the lakes or were impounded behind terminal moraines. During more recent glacial activity (i.e. Fraser Glaciation), Lake Ozette is thought to have been an important refugium for many aquatic and wetland species (Buckingham et al. 1995). Massive landslides created an earthen dam across a portion of Lake Crescent and in the process created Lake Sutherland (Williams 2002). Lake Cushman resides in glacial trough and formed when the Skokomish River was impounded from a terminal moraine. Contemporary Lake Cushman is larger than the glacially-derived lake due to the construction of a dam near its mouth. Lake Quinault sits in the glacially carved valley of the Quinault River.

The Olympic Mountains form a central core within OLYM and each of the ten major rivers on the Olympic Peninsula radiate out from glaciers, seasonal snowfields, headwater wetlands and lakes. Generally, the rivers found in the western portion of the park are broad, glacially-carved U-shaped valleys with wide floodplains while those on the north, south, and east are often embedded in confined, narrow, steep-walled valleys (NPS 2008c). The Elwha River, the largest watershed within OLYM, originates deep in the Olympic Mountains and flows north into the Strait of Juan de Fuca. In the early 20th century, two dams, one of which occurs in OLYM (Glines Canyon Dam), were constructed along the Elwha River to supply power to local communities. However, the dams destroyed one of the richest runs of salmon outside of Alaska (ten different runs of anadromous fish). In 1992, the U.S. Congress passed the Elwha River Ecosystems and Fisheries Restoration Act which aims to restore the ecological integrity of the Elwha River watershed through partnerships of the National Park Service, the Lower Elwha Klallam Tribe, local communities, and the dam owners (NPS 2008c).

The Sol Duc River drains the northeastern corner of the park with headwater located along the northern flank of Bogachiel Peak and southern flank of Mount Appleton. The Bogachiel River drains the western flank of Bogachiel Peak flowing west toward the town of Forks then further to the Pacific Ocean. The Hoh and Queets rivers drain the flanks of Mount Olympus and then flow west toward the Pacific Ocean. In the southwest corner of OLYM, the Quinault River flows toward the Pacific Ocean upon travelling down a glaciated valley from its headwaters in near the central core of the Olympic Mountains. The Bogachiel, Hoh, Queets, and Quinault river drainages all support the so-called temperate rainforests which grow along the river terraces of these glaciated valleys (NPS 2008c; Franklin and Dyrness 1988). Only the upper most tip of the Wynoochee River that drains south into Chehalis River and Grays Harbor, occurs on OLYM. The Skokomish River drains the southern flanks of Mount Duckabush and western flanks of Mounts Skokomish and Henderson before flowing into Lake Cushman and then onto the Hood Canal. The Duckabush and Dosewallips rivers both drain the eastern side of the crest of the Olympic Mountains and flow eastward into the Hood Canal. The Dungeness River drains the northeastern portion of the park and flows just west of the town of Sequim before emptying into the eastern end of the Strait of Juan de Fuca.

Land Use and Settlement History

Historical and contemporary land use can have a significant effect on the vegetation patterns found in any particular location. Continual use of vegetation by native peoples can affect vegetation patterns by controlling succession through fire and altering species composition via selective use. Significant impacts from Euro-American settlers and contemporary human use include the introduction of non-native plants, mining, dam construction, fire suppression, and widespread logging. A brief description of historical and recent land use within or affecting each park is given below.

Mount Rainier National Park

Historical use of MORA by Native American tribes such as the Nisqually, Puyallup, Squaxin Island, Muckleshoot, Yakama, and Cowlitz included seasonal use (e.g. summer and fall) to hunt, gather berries, collect medicinal plants, and gather other useful resources (NPS 2008a). Archeological evidence does not suggest that native people established permanent residence in the current MORA rather use was associated with seasonal resource extraction (Catton 1996). Many of these tribes continue to use the park today for many of the same reasons as their ancestors. As early as 15,000 to 10,000 years B.P. (before present), when much of Mount Rainier was under permanent ice, many local people lived in the lowlands surrounding Mount Rainier (NPS 2008a). As the ice began to recede between 9,000 to 8,500 years B.P., many of the contemporary vegetation patterns began to develop. Elk, deer, mountain goats and sheep, pika, bear, ptarmigan, grouse, and huckleberries were all likely important food sources for native peoples, all of which tend to be most abundant in early seral forests, shrublands, or meadows (Burtchard 1998). The subalpine and alpine zones were likely the most common place to find these habitats in abundance. Archaeological evidence suggests that by 4,000 years B.P. (and possibly much earlier) native peoples were utilizing (e.g. hunting, gathering, collecting) resources found in the mid-upper elevation forests, wetlands, and meadows (NPS 2008a). Archeological studies at MORA didn't begin in earnest until the late 1990's and at present, only about 3.5% of MORA has been inventoried (NPS 2008a). To date, over 75 archaeological sites and isolated artifacts have been documented throughout the park. These data do not provide much information about the full range of resources that were used nor do they indicate fluctuations or change in resource utilization through time (Burtchard 1998).

These studies have also revealed over 35 historic sites and isolated artifacts dating back to late 19th to early 20th century mining, recreation, and early park development. Such remains include old camp sites, trash, abandoned roadbeds, mine adits, and structural remains (NPS 2008a). Tent camps were established in this time period at Paradise to accommodate early tourists (Burtchard et al. 2008). During the mid- to late-19th century, the timber industry became established and grew with the development of the transcontinental railroad system providing a connection to eastern markets. These developments also resulted in the establishment and growth of urban centers in the region (Catton 1996). Much of MORA was set aside as a forest reserve in 1893 and thus was not subject to the intensity of timber harvest as other areas in the region (Catton 1996).

During the first four to five years after the park's creation, no more than 500 people visited the mountain each summer. Longmire and Paradise were the most popular destinations. Spray Park and Crater Lake (Mowich Lake) were also tourist destinations in the northwest portion of the park (Catton 1996). Visitor use climbed from 1,786 in 1906 to 34,814 in 1915 with most use concentrated in the southwest portion of the park (Catton 1996). Over 1.1 million tourists visited MORA in 2007 (http://www.nature.nps.gov/stats/).

North Cascades National Park Service Complex
The following discussion is adapted from NPS (2008b).
Historically, five Salishan-speaking tribes lived within NOCA. These tribes included the Nooksack, living along the Nooksack River; the Chilliwack, along the lower Chilliwack River and Chilliwack Lake; the Chelan, along the Stehekin River and Lake Chelan; the Upper Skagit, along the Skagit River below Newhalem Gorge; and the Lower Thompson, in British Columbia and along the Skagit River above the Newhalem Gorge. Native peoples used all zones of the mountains but permanently inhabited sites were limited to lowlands. Within NOCA, camps or villages have been discovered at the head of Lake Chelan, along the lower portions of the Chilliwack River, and along the Skagit River. The oldest site located is near the headwaters of the Skagit River, at Hozomeen, near the north end of what is now Ross Lake. Archaeological evidence suggests this site may have been occupied continuously or intermittently for over 8,000 years. Archaeologists are not certain whether the people living at Hozomeen are ancestors of contemporary tribes. Native peoples traveled into the mountains to trade and obtain local resources. Hunting camps, stone artifacts, and quarry sites have been found at high as 6,600 feet. Approximately 260 prehistoric sites have been identified, some dating older than 8,500 years. Mountain goats were a very important resource as they provided food and wool. Deer, elk, bear, marmots, and salmon were also important food sources. A trade network connecting people living east in the Columbia River Basin with those living west in the Puget Lowlands was established across many of the mountain passes within NOCA. For example, Cascade Pass was a crossroads for native peoples living in Lake Chelan and in the upper Skagit watershed. The Chilliwack and Lower Thompson native peoples may have used Whatcom Pass as a route across the northern portion of the North Cascades.

Commercial exploitation of the North Cascades began with fur trappers who were soon followed by miners, loggers, and builders. Fur traders were among the first Euro-Americans to explore the North Cascade region, although they are thought to have only explored lower reaches of the range. As settlement continued in the 19th century, fur trapping of beaver, bear, cougar, wolf, lynx, fisher, marten, and fox was conducted to supplement income and necessities. Exploration of the North Cascades by Euro-Americans began in the mid- to late 19th century. Although many expeditions occurred, most were restricted to major river valleys and mountain passes. In 1846, Washington Territory was opened to homesteading resulting in settlements being established along the Cascade, Skagit, and Stehekin river valleys. Most settlers made their living as shopkeepers and innkeepers for the trappers and miners who came to the area. Gold prospecting began along the Skagit River in the 1850s, and with the discovery of gold along Ruby Creek, a rush of miners descended into the valley. By 1880, miners began to focus on other minerals such as silver and lead, which were located at higher elevations. Claims were established near Cascade Pass in places such as Doubtful Lake, Boston and Horseshoe Basins, and Bridge Creek. Logging has not affected much of NOCA. However, once the natural logjam blocking along the lower Skagit River was cleared, logging operations began to work their way up the valley into the mountains. Some logging also occurred in the Stehekin Valley where small mills were established for local lumber use (e.g. apple boxes). For the most part, the absence of an adequate transportation system limited effort to expand logging over much of the NOCA landscape. Miners and settler built some roads, bridges, tunnels, and cabins throughout the area. In the early 20th century, two hydroelectric dams were built by Seattle City Light along the Skagit River: Diablo in 1930 and Ross Dam in 1940. The construction of these dams has not only impacted the aquatic environment of the river but also resulted in intensive logging in the valley. Over 81 unique and nationally recognized buildings and structures are found within the park. There are also remnants of at least 23 historic cultural landscapes within park boundaries. Vistor use is limited with less than 19,000 visitors in 2007 (http://www.nature.nps.gov/stats/).

Olympic National Park

The earliest known inhabitants of the Olympic Peninsula date back to about 13,000 years B.P. Modern native cultures became established about 4,000 to 6,000 years B.P. when contemporary vegetation patterns developed (Henderson 1989). Eight tribes are known to have been established on or utilized lands now within OLYM (NPS 2008c). These include the Hoh, Jamestown S'Klallam, Elwha Klallam, Makah, Port Gamble S'Klallam, Quileute, Quinault, and Skokomish (NPS 2008c). Archaeological studies in OLYM have been limited; however, available data suggests that native peoples likely used the high county much as those in NOCA or MORA did (McNulty 2003). The archaeological data clearly shows that native peoples developed a sophisticated culture around maritime resources. These peoples relied heavily on salmon, shell-fish, sea mammals as well as salal, huckleberries, camas, bracken fern, and salmonberry as food resources. Western redcedar was a very important resource for building materials, tools, baskets, clothing, etc. (NPS 2008c; Henderson et al. 1989). Many of these tribes still maintain their traditions. To date, about 650 archaeological sites have been documented in the park.

Euro-American settlement began in the mid-19th century. Settlement of the Olympic Peninsula occurred in the mid- to late-1800's (Henderson et al. 1989). Early settlements were mostly along the coast, near Hood Canal and present-day Port Townsend, Sequim, Port Angeles, and Neah

Bay (NPS 2008c). Some scattered homesteading occurred along some of the major river valleys, such as the Humes Ranch in OLYM (NPS 2008c). There are 130 historic structures in the park associated with early settler activity (NPS 2008c). Early logging on the Olympic Peninsula began in the northwest corner and near Grays Harbor (Henderson et al. 1989). The first sawmill was built at Port Discovery in 1858. Logging in the southern portion of the Peninsula began in the 1870's (Henderson et al. 1989). In 1885, Lieutenant J.P. O'Neil led an expedition to explore the northeastern Olympic Mountains which traveled the Dungeness drainage, Hurricane Ridge, and the Elwha River. The interior of the Olympic Mountains remained relatively unexplored by Euro-Americans until 1889 when the Press Expedition traversed up the Elwha drainage over the mountains and exited via the Quinault River (NPS 2008c). In 1890, Lieutenant O'Neil led another expedition exploring the South Fork and North Fork of the Skokomish River to O'Neil Pass. Thus, most of the interior of OLYM was relatively free of major human impacts. However, near the turn of the century, concern over excessive logging of the Olympic Peninsula was beginning to grow. The Olympic Forest Reserve was established in 1897 as a response to such concern. Twelve years later, President Theodore Roosevelt designated a portion of the reserve as Mount Olympus National Monument in order to provide further protection to the resident herd of Roosevelt elk (NPS 2008c). However, within a decade the monument size was cut in half due to pressure from the logging industry, opening much of the lowland forest to timber harvest (NPS 2008c). In 1938, President Franklin Roosevelt established Olympic National Park. In 1953, a strip of land along the coast was added to OLYM (NPS 2008c).

In 1935, 2,200 tourists visited Mount Olympus National Monument and in 1939 and that number grew to 404,125 in 1950, 2,289,200 in 1975, and 3,142,774 by 2005 (NPS 2008c). In 2005, 31,000 people spent time camping in the park's backcountry (NPS 2008c). OLYM has 16 developed campgrounds, 64 trailheads, 611 miles of hiking trail, 168 miles of road, and 457 buildings associated with the management and support of the park's resources (NPS 2008c). Visitor records for OLYM document over 3 million users in 2007, third most in the National Park system (http://www.nature.nps.gov/stats/).

Vegetation

The mild, wet climate of western Washington favors forest development. As such, the coniferous forests which dominate this region often attain a longevity and size which is unparalleled in most other forested regions of the world (Franklin and Dyrness 1988). In most mesic, temperate regions of the northern hemisphere conifers play a pioneer role in the landscape and, although they may be found in mature forests, are typically only dominant in early seral communities. However, in the Pacific Northwest, this pattern is reversed with deciduous, hardwood trees serving as the dominant early seral trees (Franklin and Dyrness 1988). This phenomenon is thought to be due to two factors: (1) historical biogeographic patterns and (2) the temporal distribution of precipitation (Franklin and Dyrness 1988). Historical climatic events may have selected the predominance of conifers from the Arcto-Tertiary forests of the Miocene (Brubaker 1991; Whitlock 1992; Franklin and Dyrness 1988). The contemporary climate of year-round mild temperatures along with a seasonal distribution of precipitation (e.g. wet winters and relatively dry summers) conveys a competitive advantage to conifers as they can continue growth through winter months as well as endure dry summer months (Franklin and Dyrness 1988). Fine-scale variation of environmental variables (e.g. soils, hydrology, aspect, geology, etc.) results in non-forested vegetation types such as wetlands, riparian areas, balds, prairies, oak woodlands, etc. Disturbances such as fire, windthrow, lahars, avalanches, flooding, insect damage, disease, and human activity all strongly affect vegetation patterns throughout the region.

Vegetation patterns in the Pacific Northwest are often described using the Forest Zone concept, which is based on the climatically defined dominance of major tree species (Franklin and Dyrness 1988; Gavin et al. 2005). For this report, we describe broad vegetation patterns found within the three parks using mid-level units of the National Vegetation Classification (NVC), specifically the Macrogroup and Group units (FGDC 2008; Table 1), which occur at roughly similar scales to the Forest Zone concept. Macrogroups are defined by moderately broad sets of diagnostic plant species and growth forms that reflect biogeographic variation in composition and sub-continental to regional differences in mesoclimate, geology, substrates, hydrology, and disturbance regimes (FGDC 2008; Table 1). Groups are defined by relatively narrow sets of diagnostic plant species, broadly similar composition, and diagnostic growth forms that reflect biogeographic variation in mesoclimate, geology, substrates, hydrology, and disturbance regimes (FGDC 2008; Table 1). In the discussion below, Forest Groups that occupy most of the landscape (e.g. matrix forests) are described for each of the three parks. Thereafter, descriptions of the smaller scale vegetation types embedded within these matrix forests are provided within the context of Macrogroups and Groups. Specific patterns of distribution of the Macrogroups and Groups are then described for each park.

At low elevations along the coast, Sitka spruce (*Picea sitchensis*), western hemlock (*Tsuga heterophylla*), and western redcedar (*Thuja plicata*) dominate forests in areas with strong maritime influence where annual precipitation is generally greater than 100 inches and summer fog predominates (Henderson et al. 1989). These forests are classified as the North Pacific Hypermaritime Sitka Spruce Forest Group or the North Pacific Hypermaritime Western Redcedar -Western Hemlock Forest Group which, collectively, are synonymous with the Sitka Spruce Zone (Franklin and Dyrness 1988). The primary difference between these two Forest Groups is the dominance of Sitka spruce (over 10% cover) in the former and the high constancy of western redcedar in the Western Redcedar -Western Hemlock Forest Group. Sitka spruce is a dominant or codominant in the North Pacific Hypermaritime Sitka Spruce Forest Group with western hemlock, and western redcedar. Bigleaf maple (*Acer macrophyllum*), and rarely Pacific silver fir (*Abies amabilis*) or Douglas-fir (*Pseudotsuga menziesii* ssp. *menziesii*) may be present as forest canopy associates. Western hemlock and western redcedar are the dominant tree species in the North Pacific Hypermaritime Western Redcedar -Western Hemlock Forest Group. Red alder (*Alnus rubra*) dominates disturbed sites within both Forest Groups. Understory species composition in both Groups varies according to local site conditions but includes red huckleberry (*Vaccinium parvifolium*), Alaska huckleberry (*Vaccinium alaskaense*), salmonberry (*Rubus spectabilis*), salal (*Gaultheria shallon*), vine maple (*Acer circinatum*), sword fern (*Polystichum munitum*), lady-fern (*Athyrium felix-femina*), oxalis (*Oxalis oregana*), false lily-of-the-valley (*Maianthemum dilatatum*), Siberian miner's lettuce (*Claytonia sibirica*), and foamflower (*Tiarella trifoliata*) (Henderson et al. 1989). Along the Hoh, Quinault, Queets, and Bogachiel River valleys, old growth temperate "rain forests" are found on old alluvial terraces. Although species composition is similar to other forests in these Groups, the temperate "rainforests" are considered distinct by some researchers due to higher rainfall (140-167 inches), the immense size of the trees, the abundance of epiphytes, and herbivory associated with Roosevelt elk (*Cervus canadensis roosevelti*) (NPS 2008c).

The most extensive low elevation forest type in western Washington, the North Pacific Maritime Douglas-fir-Western Hemlock Forest Group is dominated by Douglas-fir, western hemlock and western redcedar. These forests are synonymous with the Western Hemlock Zone of Franklin and Dyrness (1988) and occur from southern British Columbia south through the Puget Trough, low lying areas on the Olympic Peninsula, and along the base of the west Cascades. Depending on latitude, elevation of this zone ranges from sea level to approximately 3300 ft. Western hemlock is the most shade tolerant of these species and thus is the characteristic dominant of mature forests. Douglas-fir is an early, long-lived seral species in this zone. However, due to the longevity of Douglas-fir, even old growth stands have a conspicuous amount of Douglas-fir present. Western redcedar is typically found on moist to wet sites. Common understory species include salal, oceanspray (*Holodiscus discolor*), Oregongrape (*Mahonia nervosa*), Pacific rhododendron (*Rhododendron macrophyllum*), sword fern, salmonberry, vine maple, various huckleberries (*Vaccinium* spp.), and oxalis (*Oxalis oregana*). Pacific Madrone (*Arbutus menziesii*) and Oregon white-oak (*Quercus garryana*) are found in dry sites throughout the area. Lodgepole or shoreline pine (*Pinus contorta* vars. *contorta* and *latifolia*) are found on stressful sites such as dry sites, lahars, and bogs. Hardwoods such as red alder and bigleaf maple are common on disturbed sites.

In the montane regions, the North Pacific Mesic Western Hemlock-Silver Fir Forest Group is the predominant forest type. These forests, equivalent to the Silver Fir Zone (Franklin and Dyrness 1988), occur on the western slopes and isolated upper eastern slopes of the Cascades and the Olympic Mountains, except for the northeastern portion. Elevation ranges from approximately 2000 feet to 4250 feet. Pacific silver fir, western hemlock, and Douglas-fir are major dominants of this zone. Noble fir (*Abies procera*), western redcedar and rarely western white pine can be dominant although these species usually occur as minor canopy associates. Near its upper elevation limit, mountain hemlock (*Tsuga mertensiana*) and Alaska yellow-cedar (*Cupressus nootkatensis)* may be present in this Group. Geography and site conditions (e.g. wet vs. dry) results in variable composition of these forests however huckleberries, false azalea (*Menziesia ferruginea*), salal, rhododendrons, pipsissewa (*Chimaphila* spp.), wintergreen (*Pyrola* spp.), bunchberry (*Cornus unalaschkensis*), queen's cup (*Clintonia uniflora*), twinflower (*Linnaea borealis*), beargrass (*Xerophyllum tenax*), brambles (*Rubus lasiococcus, R. pedatus*) and trailing yellow violet (*Viola sempervirens*) are common under a range of moisture conditions. Foamflower, rosy twistedstalk (*Streptopus lanceolatus*), vanilla leaf (*Achlys triphylla*), oak fern (*Gymnocarpium dryopteris*), inside-out flower (*Vancouveria hexandra*), and star flowered false Solomon's seal (*Smilacina stellata*) are common in mesic sites. In the Olympic Mountains, oxalis *(Oxalis* spp.*)* and deer fern *(Blechnum spicant)* are often common understory species. Douglas-fir and/or noble fir are typical early seral trees but give way to western hemlock and Pacific silver fir over centuries.

The North Pacific Mountain Hemlock-Silver Fir Forest and Tree Island Group, which ranges from approximately 4,250 to 6,050 feet, is the highest closed forest type in western Washington. The dominant trees in this group include mountain hemlock and silver fir. Those species are often early seral trees on moist sites while lodgepole pine and subalpine fir serve the seral role on drier sites. Site temperature, moisture, and snow accumulation influence species composition of these forests. Big huckleberry (*Vaccinium membranaceum*), oval-leaf blueberry (*V. ovalifolium*), beargrass, one-sided wintergreen (*Orthilia secunda*), brambles (*Rubus lasiococcus, R. pedatus*), white rhododendron (*Rhododendron albiflorum*), false azalea, Sitka valerian (*Valeriana sitchensis*), trailing yellow violet, northwestern twayblade (*Listera caurina*), and avalanche lily (*Erythronium montanum*) are common understory species. Following fires, forest development can be slow due to harsh environmental conditions. Repeated burning of these areas leads to relatively permanent shrublands dominated by big huckleberry, mountain ash (*Sorbus* spp.), beargrass, and spiraea (*Spiraea* spp.).

At higher elevations, the North Pacific Mountain Hemlock-Silver Fir Forest and Tree Island Group and Northern Rocky Mountain Whitebark-Limber Pine Woodland Group typically appear as parklands with tree islands interspersed with extensive low shrublands and meadows. Mountain hemlock, Alaska yellow-cedar, subalpine fir, and Pacific silver fir dominate the tree islands in the North Pacific Mountain Hemlock-Silver Fir Forest and Tree Island Group. While subalpine fir, whitebark pine, subalpine larch (*Larix lyallii*), and the occasional Engelmann spruce are dominant and form woodlands and tree islands in Northern Rocky Mountain Whitebark-Limber Pine Woodland Group (limber pine (*Pinus flexilis*) does not occur in Washington but is part of this widespread floristic unit in the Rocky Mountains). Understory species in the tree islands of both Groups include many species found in adjacent meadows (i.e. the North Pacific Alpine-Subalpine Dwarf-shrubland and Heath and the Northern Rocky Mountain-Vancouverian Subalpine-Montane Mesic Herbaceous Meadow Groups) such as pink big huckleberry, mountain-heather (*Phyllodoce empetriformis*), white mountain-heather (*Cassiope mertensiana*), and blueleaf huckleberry (*Vaccinium deliciosum*). The extensive subalpine meadows are often dominated by subalpine lupine (*Lupinus arcticus* ssp. *subalpinus*), false hellebore (*Veratrum viride*), Sitka valerian, showy sedge (*Carex spectabilis*), alpine bistort (*Polygonum bistortoides*), partridgefoot (*Luetkea pectinata*), avalanche lily, and woolly pussytoes (*Antennaria lanata*) (Chappell et al. 2001). Another subalpine forest type within this group, occurs in the northeastern portion of OLYM and MORA and in NOCA. Subalpine fir (*Abies lasiocarpa*) is the dominant tree while Engelmann spruce (*Picea engelmannii*), and whitebark pine (*Pinus albicaulis*) can be codominants. Common understory species in these forests include rattlesnake plantain (*Goodyera oblongifolia*), smooth woodrush (*Luzula glabrata*), white rhododendron, false azalea (*Menziesia ferruginea*), mountain boxwood (*Paxistima myrsinites*), beargrass (*Xerophyllum tenax*), thimbleberry (*Rubus parviflorus*), and mountain ash (*Sorbus* spp.).

In contrast to the Rocky Mountains, the alpine zone in the Cascades and Olympic Mountains is limited due to a narrow belt between treeline and permanent snow/ice, as well as the steep, rugged terrain resulting in an abundance of bare rock and talus. Extreme cold, windy sites with moderate to deep snowpack form alpine environments (Chappell et al. 2001). Alpine plants have adapted to constant wind, intense solar radiation, drought, and infertile and poorly developed soils (Biek 2000). The distribution of alpine vegetation types is controlled by length of the growing season, slope, and aspect (Edwards 1980). Vegetation consists of krummholz stands of tree species which also occur in the subalpine and a mosaic of dwarf-shrublands, turf, fell-fields, and sparsely vegetated snowbed communities. This collectively comprises the North Pacific Alpine Herbaceous Meadow and the North Pacific Alpine-Subalpine Dwarf-shrubland Groups. Characteristic species include white mountain-heather, pink mountain-heather, green mountain-heather (*Phyllodoce glanduliflora*), partridgefoot, Tolmie's saxifrage (*Saxifraga tolmiei*), crowberry (*Empetrum nigrum*), common juniper (*Juniperus communis*), evergreen kinnikinnick (*Arctostaphylos uva-ursi*), shrubby cinquefoil (*Pentaphylloides floribunda*), willows (*Salix cascadensis, S. reticulata* ssp. *nivalis*), alpine fescue (*Festuca brachyphylla*), sedges (*Carex spectabilis, C. nigricans, C. breweri, C. capitata, C. nardina, C. phaeocephala, C. pseudoscirpoidea*), spreading phlox (*Phlox diffusa*), Lobb's lupine (*Lupinus sellulus* var. *lobbii*), mountain avens (*Dryas octopetala*), Piper's woodrush (*Luzula piperi*), and louseworts (*Pedicularis contorta, P. ornithorhyncha*) (Chappell et al. 2001).

Throughout each of the three parks, smaller scale vegetation types are found within the Forest Groups described above. For example, bigleaf maple, Sitka spruce, black cottonwood (*Populus balsamiferia* ssp. *trichocarpa*), red alder, Oregon ash (*Fraxinus latifolia*), salmonberry, devil's club (*Oplopanax horridus*) and a variety of other shrubs and herbaceous species are characteristic of the North Pacific Lowland Riparian Forest and Woodland Group (Chappell 1999). Riparian groups are in typically well-drained areas with overbank flooding, groundwater discharge or high water tables associated with flowing water. The North Pacific Lowland-Montane Riparian and Wet Slope Shrubland Group occurs at higher elevations and is dominated by mountain alder (*Alnus incana* ssp. *tenuifolia*), Sitka alder (*A. viridis* ssp. *sinuata*), Booth's willow (*Salix boothii*), undergreen willow (*S. commutata*), Sierran willow (*S. eastwoodiae*), and blueberries (*Vaccinium uliginosum* or *V. deliciosum*). Red alder and western redcedar, along with understory species such as deer fern (*Blechnum spicant*), skunk cabbage (*Lysichiton americanum*), slough sedge (*Carex obnupta*), salmonberry, and water-parsley (*Oenanthe sarmentosa*) dominate the North Pacific Hardwood-Conifer Swamp Group which mostly occurs at low elevations. The North Pacific Lowland Bog and Fen Group is found at low elevations in poorly drained river valleys, along lakes and in depressions throughout western Washington where various species of sedges (*Carex* spp.), ericaceous shrubs (*Kalmia microphylla, Ledum groenlandicum, Vaccinium oxycoccos*, etc.), and *Sphagnum* moss predominate (Kulzer et al. 2001). Shore pine (*Pinus contorta* var. *contorta*), sweet gale (*Myrica gale*), and hardhack (*Spiraea douglasii*) are occasionally found in these peatlands. The North Pacific Montane Fen Group also occurs in the subalpine zone. These peatlands are dominated by variety of species including bog-laurel (*Kalmia microphylla*), sedges (e.g. *Carex aquatilis, C. utriculata, C. echinata* ssp. *echinata*), Thurber's bentgrass (*Agrostis thurberiana*), cottongrass (*Eriophorum* spp.), tufted clubrush (*Trichophorum cespitosum*), marsh violet (*Viola palustris*), northern star flower (*Trientalis arctica*), Oregon saxifrage (*Saxifraga oregana*), elephant head (*Pedicularis groenlandica*) as well as *Sphagnum* and brown mosses (Chappell et al. 2001). The Temperate Pacific Freshwater Emergent Marsh Group is abundant throughout western Washington and is comprised of sedges (*Carex* spp.), bulrushes (*Scirpus* and *Schoenoplectus* spp.), cattail (*Typha latifolia*), spike-rushes (*Eleocharis* spp.), rushes (*Juncus* spp.), burreeds (*Sparganium* spp.), pondweeds (*Potamogeton* spp.), various grasses, and aquatic plants (Chappell et al. 2001). In the subalpine, the Temperate Pacific Subalpine-Montane Wet Meadow Group is interspersed in throughout the subalpine parklands and dominated by marsh marigold (*Caltha leptosepala*), tufted hairgrass (*Deschampsia caespitosa*), bluejoint reedgrass (*Calamagrostis canadensis*), black sedge (*Carex nigricans*), Holm's Rocky Mountain sedge (*C. scopulorum*), Sitka sedge (*C. aquatilis* var. *dives*), and Northwest territory sedge (*C. utriculata*) (Chappell et al. 2001).

Small patch upland vegetation types include the North Pacific Hypermaritime Shrub and Herbaceous Headland Group located along the outer coast in OLYM subject to strong winds and salt spray that result in a stressful environment supporting small grasslands in a mosaic with stunted trees and shrublands. Shrubs such as salal, crowberry *(Empetrum nigrum)*, evergreen huckleberry (*Vaccinium ovatum*) are common along with grasses such as (*Calamagrostis nutkaensis*) and Sitka brome (*Bromus sitchensis*) (Rust 1992; Chappell et al. 2001). The North Pacific Herbaceous Bald and Bluff Group appear in the lowland up into the montane. This Group consists of distinct, small patches of non-forested areas within the forest matrix which occur on steep slopes with relatively shallow soils overlaying a restrictive layer of bedrock (Chappell 2006). Balds are dominated by herbaceous vegetation, dwarf-shrubs, and/or mosses and lichens and are often fringed by Vancouverian Dry Douglas-fir-(Madrone) Forest and Woodland Group (Chappell 2006). Talus or scree slopes (e.g. North Pacific Montane Massive Bedrock, Cliff, and Talus Group) have variable composition but vine maple, oceanspray, trailing snowberry (*Symphoricarpos hesperius*), parsley fern (*Cryptogramma crispa*), beaked hazelnut (*Corylus cornuta* var. *californica*), and redstem ceanothus (*Ceanothus sanguineus*) are common associates. Snow creep and/or avalanches maintain shrublands dominated by Sitka alder (*Alnus sinuata*). Due to frequent avalanches these shrublands are fairly stable with Alaska yellow-cedar being the only tree to survive in these areas. Forbs are often abundant in these shrublands due to high moisture levels.

Mount Rainier National Park

Spatial and temporal climatic variation, volcanism, glacier activity, elevation changes (gradient of over 12,000 feet), large-scale disturbances (fire, windthrow, insects, avalanches, etc.) and various geologic substrates and soils types have resulted in a rich diversity of vegetation across relatively short distances at MORA (NPS 2008a). This diversity is expressed both in the number of plant species (over 890 vascular and 260 non-vascular plant and fungi species) as well as in the diversity of plant associations. More than 100 exotic plant species also occur in MORA, mostly along transportation corridors, near trails and campsites, and along riparian corridors (NPS 2008a).

Approximately 58 percent of the park is forested. Temperature, moisture (including snowfall), and disturbance regimes are strong determinants of the type of forest found in any given site (Franklin et al. 1988). The age of individual forest stands varies according to the time since the last major disturbance. Stands less than 100 years old occur on moraines left by receding glaciers, mudflows, or burned areas while 1,000 year old-growth stands occur in areas protected from disturbances in the Ohanapecosh, Cowlitz, Nisqually, and Carbon River drainages (Franklin et al. 1988). Summer moisture regimes appear to have a strong influence on the patterns of forest types in the lowlands (Franklin et al. 1988).

The North Pacific Maritime Douglas-fir-Western Hemlock Forest Group occurs from the park's boundary at 1,700 feet to approximately 3,000 feet in elevation and is best developed in the major river valleys (Biek 2000). One of the few examples of an inland temperate rainforest (similar to those found in the North Pacific Hypermaritime Sitka Spruce Forest Group) is found in the northwest portion of the park in the Carbon River drainage (Biek 2000). The North Pacific Mesic Western Hemlock-Silver Fir Forest Group, the characteristic forest type for MORA, is found up to about 4,700 feet. These forests are found on level to steep topography. Pacific silver fir, Alaska yellow-cedar, western white pine, and noble fir are characteristic species. These forests have a closed canopy but shorter and fewer understory shrubs and less cover of herbaceous species giving it a more open appearance than the North Pacific Maritime Douglas-fir-Western Hemlock Forest Group forests (Biek 2000). The North Pacific Mountain Hemlock-Silver Fir Forest and Tree Island Group occur in the subalpine and extends up to about 7,000 feet with closed forests giving way to subalpine parklands (mosaic of tree islands and meadows) usually between 4,500 feet to 5,000 feet and subalpine parklands transition into alpine environment around 7,000 feet (NPS 2008a). The depth and duration of snowpack strongly influences forest patterns in the North Pacific Mesic Western Hemlock-Silver Fir Forest and North Pacific Mountain Hemlock-Silver Fir Forest and Tree Island Groups (Franklin et al. 1988).

The subalpine parklands extend up to about 7,000 feet and occupy about 23 percent of the park. The meadows found in MORA's subalpine parklands have been clustered into two Groups and, as with the forest communities, are associated with the depth and duration of snowpack: (1) North Pacific Alpine-Subalpine Dwarf-shrubland and Heath Group, which are dominated by ericaceous shrubs such as mountain heather (*Phyllodoce* or *Cassiope*) or huckleberry (*Vaccinium* spp.); and (2) Northern Rocky Mountain-Vancouverian Subalpine-Montane Mesic Herbaceous Meadow Group which includes a) lush herbaceous meadows dominated by tall perennials such as Sitka valerian, subalpine lupine, showy sedge, and green hellebore (*Veratrum viride*), b) low herbaceous meadows dominated by fan-leaved cinquefoil (*Potentilla flabellifolia*), pussytoes (*Antennaria* spp.), and black sedge (*Carex nigricans*), and c) dry grasslands dominated by green fescue (*Festuca viridula*) and subalpine lupine located on well-drained sites more common on the east side of the park (Henderson 1974; Franklin et al. 1988). The Temperate Pacific Subalpine-Montane Wet Meadow Group dominated by sedges along with alpine aster (*Oreostemma alpigenum*) and pussytoes also occurs in these parklands.

The alpine environment extends from the upper limit of the subalpine parklands to Mount Rainier's summit. Approximately 50 percent of the alpine is covered by permanent snow and ice and glacier-modified bedrock (North Pacific Alpine and Subalpine Bedrock and Scree) while the remaining area is dominated by sparse to open alpine vegetation of the North Pacific Alpine-Subalpine Dwarf-shrubland and Heath and the North Pacific Alpine Herbaceous Meadow Groups. This vegetation includes: (1) fell-fields which consist of small rocks on gentle slopes. The rocks provide protected niches where sedges, golden fleabane (*Erigeron aureus*), Lobb's lupine, spreading phlox, mountain avens, Piper's woodrush, penstemons (*Penstemon* spp.), and louseworts; (2) snowbeds have the shortest growing season and some may not be snow-free every year. Tolmie's saxifrage, Shasta buckwheat (*Eriogonum pyrolifolium*) or Piper's woodrush are typical dominate species of snowbeds; and (3) dwarf-heath shrublands are the oldest known plant communities in MORA with some thought to have persisted for up to 10,000 years. Pink mountain-heather, green mountain-heather, white mountain-heather, and black crowberry are common dominant species (Chappell et al. 2001; Edwards 1980). Green fescue also occurs as fairly extensive grasslands above treeline in the northeastern part of the park.

North Cascades National Park Service Complex
Complex geology, climate, topography, aspect, and elevation have resulted in NOCA supporting the highest diversity of vascular plants (over 1,630 species) found in any of the National Parks in the United States (NPS 2008b). Those abiotic factors also result in a variety of vegetation types. Temperature and moisture regimes have a strong influence on the distribution of forest types in NOCA. The width of the Cascade Range within NOCA creates rainshadow effects observed

even west of the Cascade Crest. Thus, in addition to species typically found in the forests of western Washington, many plant species and communities more characteristic of the mountains of eastern Washington are found within the park (Agee and Kertis 1987). The Upper Skagit-Ross Lake area within the park is well known for the convergence of coastal species with those more typical of the interior mountains (Franklin and Dyrness 1988). Slopes on the west side of Ross Lake exhibit a vegetation sequence characteristic of western Washington while slopes on the east side of Ross Lake and in the upper Lake Chelan area show forest patterns typical of the drier interior forest types. Groups with strong Rocky Mountain floristic components typically found at NOCA include the Northern Rocky Mountain Douglas-fir-Pine Forest, Northern Rocky Mountain Ponderosa Pine Woodland, East Cascades Mesic Grand fir-Douglas-fir Forest, Northern Rocky Mountain Whitebark-Limber Pine Woodland, Rocky Mountain Subalpine Dry-Mesic Spruce-Fir Forest and Woodland, and Rocky Mountain Subalpine Mesic-Wet Spruce-Fir Forest and Woodland Groups (Agee and Kertis 1987; Franklin and Dyrness 1988).

Matrix Forest Groups in NOCA are presented in the order encountered along a west to east trajectory (unless otherwise noted, this summary is adapted from Douglas (1969)). The North Pacific Maritime Douglas-fir-Western Hemlock Forest Group is found in lowlands up to about 2,500 feet and even higher on south-facing dry slopes. In addition to the species previously described for this Group, paper birch (*Betula papyrifera*), a species not found south of Everett, Washington, appears throughout these forests in NOCA (Arno and Hammerly 2007). Impressive old-growth western redcedar stands are found on alluvial terraces of Big Beaver, Little Beaver, Baker, and Chilliwack Creeks in the park (Miller and Miller 1970). The North Pacific Mesic Western Hemlock-Silver Fir Forest Group occurs in the park between 2,500 to 4,200 feet on north slopes and up to about 5,200 feet on south slopes. In valleys with substantial cold-air drainage, these forests can extend below 2,500 feet. As at Mount Rainier National Park, this Forest Group is the most extensive forest type in NOCA and is even found east of the Cascade crest in the Upper Lake Chelan area. The North Pacific Mountain Hemlock-Silver Fir Forest and Tree Island Forest Group is found above 4,200 feet on north slopes and above 5,200 feet on south slopes. However, the upper limit is variable due to very steep topography and microclimates. For example, the highest noted treeline noted in NOCA is at approximately 6,500 feet. These forests are also found on both sides of the Cascade crest in the Lake Chelan area.

The North Pacific Alpine-Subalpine Dwarf-shrubland and Heath, Northern Rocky Mountain-Vancouverian Subalpine-Montane Mesic Herbaceous Meadow, and Temperate Pacific Subalpine-Montane Wet Meadow Groups intermingle with the North Pacific Mountain Hemlock-Silver Fir Forest and Tree Island and Northern Rocky Mountain Whitebark-Limber Pine Woodland Groups to form the characteristic subalpine parklands and meadows. The alpine in NOCA is extremely fragmented and most occurrences are small due to very steep topography. In addition to krummholz, heath shrublands (*Phyllodoce* ssp. and *Cassiope mertensiana*) associated with the North Pacific Alpine-Subalpine Dwarf-shrubland and Heath and North Pacific Alpine Herbaceous Meadow Groups are a major component of the alpine in NOCA. East of the high ridges in NOCA, forests typical of eastern Washington begin to dominate the landscape. The Northern Rocky Mountain Whitebark-Limber Pine Woodland Group is the first to appear (at high elevation) heading east. In the upper Lake Chelan area, North Pacific Mesic Western Hemlock-Silver Fir and Northern Rocky Mountain Douglas-fir-Pine Forest Groups occur below subalpine forests. The Northern Rocky Mountain Douglas-fir-Pine Forest Group, found in the Ross Lake and Lake Chelan areas of NOCA, occurs along valley, stream terraces, and lower south slopes. Ponderosa pine (*Pinus ponderosa*) and Douglas-fir are early seral species. Douglas-fir dominates south slopes while grand fir dominates mesic areas. In north facing drainages, Douglas-fir, grand fir, western hemlock, western redcedar, and western white pine can co-occur as dominants.

Olympic National Park

As with the other parks, climate, topography, and elevation strongly influence vegetation patterns at OLYM. There are 1,452 species, subspecies, and varieties of plant species found on the Olympic Peninsula and the region supports 28% of the rare species tracked by the Washington Natural Heritage Program (Buckingham et al. 1995). The steep environmental gradients found in the area also support a diverse array of vegetation types.

The low elevation coastal portion of the park is dominated by the North Pacific Hypermaritime Sitka Spruce and North Pacific Hypermaritime Western Redcedar -Western Hemlock Forest Groups, both of which are found along the narrow coastal plain between the Pacific Ocean and Olympic Mountains. These forests are found below 500 feet along the coastal strip of OLYM and can reach up to 2000 feet in the river valleys on the western slope of the Olympic Mountains. These forest Groups occupy approximately 10% of OLYM (UNEP 2008). The mild climate in these areas results in extremely lush forests with dense, exuberant understory growth and an abundance of bryophytes (NPS 2008c). The North Pacific Lowland Bog and Fen Group is occasionally found along the coastal plain. The North Pacific Hypermaritime Shrub and Herbaceous Headland Group is found along the coast and is dominated by various shrubs, herbaceous species and scattered krummholz-like Sitka spruce trees (and the occasional Douglas-fir, western hemlock, or red alder) (Chappell et al. 2001).

The North Pacific Maritime Douglas-fir-Western Hemlock Forest Group occurs at the base of the Olympic Mountains in very wet to dry habitats and occupy about 10% of OLYM (UNEP 2008; Henderson et al. 1989). These forests have a much broader elevation range on the drier, east-side of the Peninsula where they can reach up to about 4,000 feet while in wetter areas they typically only reach up to about 2,000 feet and thus have a much narrower range (Henderson et al. 1989). On the western and wetter side of the Olympic Mountains, the North Pacific Maritime Douglas-fir-Western Hemlock Forest Group differs from other areas in western Washington by the predominance of western redcedar and western hemlock, widely scattered silver fir, and relatively low abundance of Douglas-fir. The North Pacific Mesic Western Hemlock-Silver Fir Forest Group is the major forest type, approximately 50% of the park and occurs between 2,000 and 4,000 feet. A few very old Douglas-fir trees (700+ years) are found within these forests in the wetter portion of the park and indicate an earlier and drier climate (McNulty 2003). The North Pacific Mesic Western Hemlock-Silver Fir Forest Group is absent from dry, south-facing slopes in the northeastern portion of the park, generally between 1,805 to 3,609 feet, and instead are dominated by forests similar to the Vancouverian Dry Douglas-fir-(Madrone) Forest and Woodland Group (Henderson et al. 1989; UNEP 2008). These forests are dominated by Douglas-fir that can contain small amounts of grand fir, lodgepole pine, seaside juniper (*Juniperus maritima*), or Pacific madrone (Henderson et al. 1989).

Except for the northeastern portion of OLYM, the subalpine, areas between 4,000 to about 6,000 feet, is dominated by the North Pacific Mountain Hemlock-Silver Fir Forest and Tree Island Forest Group. This forest Group occupies 20% of the park and includes the subalpine parklands (Henderson et al. 1989; UNEP 2008). As in the other two parks, the North Pacific Alpine-Subalpine Dwarf-shrubland and Heath, Northern Rocky Mountain-Vancouverian Subalpine-Montane Mesic Herbaceous Meadow, and Temperate Pacific Subalpine-Montane Wet Meadow Groups intermingle with the North Pacific Mountain Hemlock-Silver Fir Forest and Tree Island Group to form characteristic subalpine parklands and meadows. A notable spruce-fir forest type occupies the northeastern portion of the subalpine that is dominated by subalpine fir and/or lodgepole pine along with occasional whitebark pine and mountain hemlock (Henderson et al. 1989).

The North American Alpine Ice Field, North Pacific Alpine and Subalpine Bedrock and Scree, and North Pacific Alpine-Subalpine Dwarf-shrubland and Heath, and North Pacific Alpine Herbaceous Meadow Groups dominate the alpine zone which occupies approximately 10% of the park and is generally found above 6,000 feet. The vegetated portion of alpine is generally found below 7,382 feet where steep topography and permanent ice limit vegetation growth. Alpine vegetation is characterized by heath dwarf-shrublands, mat-forming, low shrubs dominated by spreading phlox, and turfs dominated by showy and black sedges.

Previous Vegetation Studies

Mount Rainier National Park
Botanical exploration over the past two centuries in MORA provide many citations from the late 1800's and early 1900's (NPS 2008a). Although Archibald Menzies, John Scouler, and David Douglas had conducted floristic surveys of western Washington the in late 18th and early 19th centuries, it was not until 1833 that William Tolmie collected plants within MORA boundaries (Biek 2000). Charles Pickering and W.D. Brackenridge, botanists associated with the Wilkes Expedition, botanized extensively up the White River to Naches Pass providing the first compilation of plants for the region near MORA (Biek 2000). Charles Piper extensively studied the flora in the region of Mount Rainier in the late 1880's. Piper published his findings in a series of articles titled "The Flora of Mount Rainier" in *The Mazama* in 1902 in which he documented 295 species (Biek 2000). In 1929, the National Park Service initiated a systematic effort to build an herbarium for the park. George Jones published the first comprehensive flora of the park, *The Flowering Plants and Ferns of Mount Rainier*, in 1938 which included 729 species. In 1983, Peter Dunwiddie listed 804 species as occurring in the park in his dissertation entitled "Holocene Forest Dynamics on Mount Rainier, Washington" (Biek 2000). The latest compilation occurs in *Flora of Mount Rainier National Park*, by David Biek (2000).

In response to concerns of human impacts to subalpine meadows, Frank Brockman conducted an ecological study of the meadows in 1959-1960 to determine the effects of foot traffic on the subalpine vegetation communities (NPS 2008a). Additional research by Hamman (1972), Henderson (1974), Edwards (1980), and NPS Science Advisor, Regina Rochefort (Rochefort and Peterson 1996) has contributed much knowledge about the ecology of subalpine and alpine meadows.

In 1975 through 1980, Franklin et al. (1988) classified and mapped Mount Rainier's forests. This research defined fourteen types of mature forests and five early seral forest types. This work has had a significant influence on management decisions within the park, especially those associated with fire management and development planning (NPS 2008a). Some other ecological studies include Hemstrom and Franklin's (1982) study of fire and disturbance ecology of the park's forests, Frehner's (1957) work on soil development and vegetation succession on the Kautz Creek mudflow, Dunwiddie's (1983) research on Holocene forest dynamics, and Cushman's (1981) study on the influence of recurrent avalanches on vegetation patterns (Biek 2000). Vegetation classification research on lands adjacent to MORA also provide insight into vegetation patterns in the park (del Moral and Long 1977; Henderson et al. 1992). The citations above only provide a brief overview of the research which has been and continues to be conducted at MORA.

North Cascades National Park Service Complex
In 1892, E.R. Lake and W.R. Hull collected plants in the upper end of Lake Chelan and at Cascades Pass (Alverson and Arnett 1986). Kirk Whited made collections near Stehekin in 1901 and David Griffith and J.R. Cotton collected around Stehekin in 1908. Harold St. John botanized and collected in the Lake Chelan area in 1924. George Ward made extensive collections in the early 1940 for his *Flora of Chelan County* (Alverson and Arnett 1986). Dorothy and Ralph Naas have made extensive collections throughout the North Cascades. Alverson and Arnett (1986) documented 665 species in the Lake Chelan-Sawtooth Ridge area. In 2002, NOCA contracted with the University of Washington Herbarium to organize a series of plant collecting trips to generate vouchers of the park's flora. From 2002-2005, 465 taxa were collected at NOCA and nearly 23% of these taxa represent new voucher records for the NOCA herbarium (NPS 2008b).

Vegetation studies in the region begin in 1962 when the U.S. Forest Service established permanent monitoring plots in the Lake Chelan-Sawtooth Ridge area to determine grazing effects on subalpine vegetation (Alverson and Arnett 1986). Franklin and Trappe (1963) provided a general description of vegetation patterns in the North Cascade range. Douglas (1969) conducted a vegetation survey of NOCA and provided a preliminary vegetation classification of the park. In the early 1970's, Douglas continued extensive ecological study of NOCA vegetation communities, including a survey of potential natural areas (Douglas 1971) and classification and ecological investigations of subalpine-alpine communities (Douglas 1972; Douglas and Bliss 1977). High elevation vegetation communities of the North Cascades range were also studied by del Moral and colleagues, who conducted work in the Alpine Lake region (del Moral et al. 1976) and Enchantment Lake Basin (del Moral 1979). Ron Taylor and George Douglas studied the natural history and vegetation ecology of Chowder Ridge near Mount Baker (Taylor and Douglas 1977) and Alverson and Arnett (1986) described vegetation types in the Lake Chelan-Sawtooth Ridge area. Agee and Kertis (1987) published a summary of the vegetation studies which accompanied the development of a cover type map for the park, in which they identify 18 cover types. Two U.S. Forest Service plant association field guides include portions of the North Cascade region have contributed much knowledge about the vegetation types within and near NOCA. These include the plant association field guide for the Mount Baker-Snoqualmie National Forest (Henderson et al. 1992) and the guide for the Wenatchee National Forest (Lillybridge et al. 1995). Grizzly Bear Habitat analysis work involved vegetation analysis and classification plant communities (Almack et al. 1993). A recent ecological study of montane wetlands in the North Cascades has also advanced vegetation ecology in the region (Risyold and Fonda 2001).

Olympic National Park

Archibald Menzies was the first botanist to explore the Olympic Peninsula in 1792. David Douglas apparently botanized in the eastern portion of the peninsula near the Hood Canal in the early 1800's and John Scouler collected from the "Straits of Juan de Fuca" in the 1820's and thus likely was in the northern part of the peninsula (Henderson et al. 1989). Charles Pickering and W.D. Brackenridge, botanists associated with the Wilkes expedition of 1841, collected in the northeastern portion of the peninsula. Louis Henderson, a botanist associated with the O'Neil expedition, was the first botanist to explore the interior of the Olympic Mountains. J.B. Flett botanized the Olympic Mountains in 1895 and L.H. Lamb collected in the southwest portion of the Olympic Peninsula in 1897 (Henderson et al. 1989). C.V. Piper surveyed the Olympic Mountains in 1890 and 1895 and included his and others collections in his 1906 "Flora of Washington." George Neville Jones extensively explored the Olympic Peninsula from 1923-1935 and based on that work as well as the work of earlier botanists described the flora for the Olympic Peninsula (Henderson et al. 1989). Buckingham et al. (1995) have provided the most recent checklist of vascular plants occurring on the Olympic Peninsula.

The first ecological description of vegetation in the Olympic Peninsula was published in George Jones' 1936 manuscript where he used the Merriam Life Zone concept to describe vegetation patterns in the region. Fonda and Bliss (1969) developed the first plant association classification for forests of the Olympic Mountains and Kuramoto and Bliss (1970) did the same for subalpine meadows. Fonda (1974) described forest succession on river terraces in OLYM. Kratz (1975) conducted a classified vegetation types within the Sitka Spruce Zone of OLYM. Belsky and del Moral (1982) studied the ecology of subalpine-alpine meadows. Henderson et al. (1989) published a classification of the forested plant associations of the Olympic National Forest. More recently, Bigley and Hull (1995) developed a forested plant association classification and Chappell (1999) initiated a classification of low-elevation riparian vegetation for the Olympic Experimental State Forest.

Methods

The methods used in this project were designed to build upon existing vegetation classification efforts in the Pacific Northwest. The project incorporates and re-evaluates 1) legacy data from previous vegetation studies and 2) new data collected by National Park Service mapping crews. Collection of new data in the parks was designed to fill known gaps in the existing classification, to document the occurrence of known associations, and to identify previously unrecognized associations. This iterative process first required that a preliminary classification and key for use by the field crews be synthesized from previous classification efforts. The subsequent collection of new data was used to update and refine the next version of the classification. An initial classification was compiled in 2005, intermediate classifications in 2006 and 2007, followed by the final classification in 2008.

Preliminary Classification

The 2005 preliminary classification was developed using three major sources of plant associations; 1) the 2005 coastal forests correlation project (CFCP Meidinger et al. 2005), 2) the 2005 version of the NVC/IVC International Vegetation Classification (FDGC 2008, NatureServe 2005) and 3) the WNHP state vegetation classification.

The 2005 preliminary classification included all plant associations recognized by NatureServe (2005), as well as new associations and future revisions to NatureServe (2005) from the coastal forests correlation project (CFCP) (Meidinger et al. 2005). The CFCP quantitatively compared plant associations from southeastern Alaska south to southwestern Oregon. Data sets of previously defined plant associations were collected into a single database and then compared with similarity indices and constancy/cover tables. A group of ecologists with regional expertise in vegetation classification reviewed the analyses and made proposals for combining and naming plant associations on this rangewide scale. C. Chappell, one of the primary authors of the CFCP, wrote short summary descriptions tailored to the three parks for associations which did not already have a summary written by NatureServe. He used CFCP vegetation tables and associated regional publications for environmental information. He edited existing NatureServe global summary descriptions of IVC/NVC plant associations to better reflect how they occur in the three parks.

The WNHP state vegetation classification includes citations of all plant associations described in Washington. The list of plant associations described in the state by all authors for associations was reviewed for potential associations likely to occur in one or more of the three parks and not already on the list of IVC/NVC and CFCP Correlation associations. Those associations recognized within the state, but not globally by NatureServe were included in the preliminary classification for the three parks. In addition, some NatureServe shrubland and herbaceous vegetation types were revised based on a recent correlation of all associations described in publications and reports for the subalpine and alpine zones in Washington.

Using the approach described above, preliminary summary descriptions were written for 192 upland types (including all physiognomic classes) and forested wetland types. Additionally, a list of the names of 50 shrub and herbaceous wetland associations likely in the parks was compiled. A preliminary key to upland associations was prepared to support field sampling.

Field Methods

Field Sampling Approach

With only two field seasons allocated to classification sampling, a targeted approach to sampling was developed that directed NPS field crews to sample in areas or vegetation types known to be gaps in the legacy data and previous vegetation classification work in the region. In 2005, Chris Chappell with the WNHP provided the following prioritization scheme to direct the field sampling. High priority areas included; shrublands, particularly avalanche chutes; Douglas-fir forests west of the Cascade Crest with no or little western hemlock or western redcedar (less than 10% cover); forests and woodlands in the Ross Lake area of NOCA dominated or co-dominated by Douglas-fir, ponderosa pine, and/or lodgepole pine; subalpine parkland tree islands/stringers west of the Cascade Crest; western redcedar-dominated upland stands with little to no western hemlock; herbaceous or dwarf-shrub "balds" west of the Cascade Crest, and dry grasslands below the subalpine zone. Medium priority areas included riparian forests (riverine floodplain or terraces), non-forested wetlands, especially middle elevations, ponderosa pine- dominated stands and bigleaf maple stands. The descriptions included in the preliminary classification also indicated when a provisional or temporary association needed more data for clarification.

Plot Data Collection

The plot data collection methods combined guidance from the NPS Vegetation Mapping Program Field Methods for Vegetation Mapping (TNC and ESRI 1994a), WNHP data collection protocols, and methods used by the USFS (Henderson and Lesher, 2003).

The basic plot survey method instructed crews to establish a fixed radius plot, the size of which scaled depending on vegetation structure. Forest plots had an area of 400 m2, shrub plots were 100 m2 and dwarf shrub, herbaceous and sparse plots were 50 m2. Within the plot, the crews recorded a suite of environmental variables including aspect, slope, elevation, landform, microposition, macroposition and topographic moisture, which is a moisture availability index that relates slope configuration (e.g. convex or concave) at the plot scale to relative slope position at the mountain scale (Henderson and Lesher 2003). When appropriate, the crews noted wetland type and hydrologic regime. A shallow hole was dug for soil characterization and texture and color was recorded by horizon.

Vegetation characterization included selecting physiognomic class, leaf type and phenology and recording the cover of dominant species by vertical layers (strata). The crews recorded an association name when possible. For undescribed types the field crew assigned a preliminary name. They also recorded feedback on the adequacy of field key and descriptions. The core of the classification plot data is the ocular species list. The crews recorded crown cover (in classes) by species for all species seen in the plot. Cover of a bryophyte species was recorded when cover was greater than 1%. Bryophytes growing on logs were excluded from cover estimates. Additional details on sampling methodology can be found in the Guide for Field Sampling (Appendix G). Examples of the field forms used in sampling are included in Appendix G.

Legacy Data

NPS staff initially acquired legacy plot data and summarized their metadata. The WNHP staff evaluated the summarized metadata to determine if the plot data were appropriate for vegetation classification. The criteria used for inclusion in classification plot data included the following: 1) a near complete vascular species list, 2) plot size scaled to vegetation type (e.g. larger for forests), and 3) cover values for all vascular species. These criteria reflect the minimal standard as discussed in Jennings et al (2002). Nine of twenty nine available legacy data sets evaluated met the criteria for classification (Appendix E). Five data sets are in OLYM and four in MORA or immediately adjacent to and east of MORA and NOCA.

The initial (2006) classification analysis included 2083 plots: 1956 legacy plots and 127 map validation plots from NPS crews. The final classification evaluated 3396 plots: 2479 legacy plots and 917 classification plots from NPS crews.

Observation Points

Legacy plots were used as observation plots when enough information was available to establish a plot into an association but insufficient data was available to describe the vegetation. One MORA data set (Franklin, et al. 1988) lacking tree cover data were classified by estimating relative cover of tree species from tree density by diameter classes. Within this MORA dataset plots in which diagnostic tree species was not clearly exceeding a threshold value or dominance criteria were not used. NPS crews collected new observation points to document the presence and range of previously described associations.

Classification Data Analysis

Plot data is managed in VPRO, developed and managed by the Ministry of Forests, Research Branch (MacKenzie and Klassen 1999). VPRO was designed for British Columbia research ecologists for managing and classifying large bodies of ecological data using standard classification techniques. This Microsoft ACCESS© program allows for tracking plots with species and environmental data, creates stand and synthesis tables, and exports data into the analytical program PC-ORD.

The 2005 classification served as the basis for developing the 2006, 2007 and final classification. It provided structure for initial plot data classification and a basis for comparison of new associations derived from the data. The regionwide CPFC was the basis for classification of forest types as identified and described by Meidinger et al. (2005). Plots were sorted into clusters that fell within the variation of the coastal correlation units using floristic indicators and environmental characteristics described in supporting literature and preliminary keys. Synthesis tables for plots assigned to these pre-existing associations were generated from VPRO and were then subjectively compared to coastal correlation tables and to published tables from supporting literature. Plots not clearly identifiable to pre-existing literature types were analyzed following the general procedure below:

1. subset data into physiognomic groupings of tree-dominated (>25% tree cover), shrub-dominated, dwarf shrub-dominated, herbaceous-dominated, and sparsely vegetated (<25% total vascular plant cover) with VPRO;
2. subdivide lifeform clusters by PCA or other clustering technique,
3. evaluate subdivisions with TWINSPAN and/or stand table manipulation;
4. compare clusters to preliminary and pre-existing classification of NPS units, NatureServe or other types in existing literature;
5. reiterate process assigning plot individually to plant association; and
6. summarize plots per determined type.

New or edited summary descriptions were written for all upland types and forested wetland types. Shrub and herbaceous wetlands and riparian communities are compiled in a list of names of associations organized with by wetland type with little other descriptive information. Descriptions of selected, widespread intermittently flooded and wet meadow associations in alpine and subalpine environments are described.

Following each field season feedback from field crews on the efficacy of preliminary classification and field keys was incorporated into the next iteration of classification. WNHP met with NPS staff to discuss experiences of the field crews and to keep mutually-agreeable progress moving forward. Each year a list of sampling priorities for vegetation classification plots needs were provided for field collection planning to verify type occurrence and increase sampling its range of variation and to sample poorly classified vegetation types, for example, upland shrublands. Field crews were directed to a prioritized sampling scheme, with first priority going towards sampling ecological types that were not well-represented in the current classification (such as dry Douglas-fir forests or avalanche chutes) and associations considered "new" or "ill-defined." Second priority areas were selected to confirm presence and expand range for types that have been described elsewhere but are not known to occur in the parks or have low sample size from the parks, and third priority was to document the occurrence and geographic range of associations that had been described for the region from these parks. In this process, crews were testing the existing key and descriptions.

The 2006 and 2007 field seasons focused on verifying and developing each year's preliminary vegetation classification for MORA, NOCA and OLYM. Each year's preliminary classification incorporated both legacy data from previous vegetation studies on the parks and newly acquired field data collected by NPS crews in the previous year. The plant association classification was complied in a format that could be used by crews to identify plant associations in the field and test the classification.

Alliance is the mapping standard for NPS projects. Alliances are vegetation classification units containing one or more associations and are defined by a characteristic range of species composition, habitat conditions, physiognomy, and diagnostic species, typically at least one of which is found in the uppermost or dominant stratum of the vegetation. NatureServe, in a separate project, will provide the classification and definition of alliances for MORA, NOCA and OLYM. That NatureServe project clusters associations defined in this report into all the revised hierarchical levels in the 2008 FGDC NVC standard. Appendix A arranges associations according to the revised hierarchy. This is the first application of the 2008 NVC hierarchy

(FGDC 2008) to a NPS classification and consequently, the hierarchical organization of the associations in this report is expected to change. The arrangement listed below reflects the hierarchical status developed by NatureServe and partners as of March 31, 2009. Future changes in the classification hierarchy will be available from NatureServe as they are modified (http://www.natureserve.org/explorer/index.htm). The forested portions of the hierarchy was better developed at that date and will likely change less than the non-forest types.

Assessment of State Rarity

A global and state ranking system developed by NatureServe and the Natural Heritage programs is used to estimate conservation priorities. The ranking system facilitates a quick assessment of an entity's rarity. An association is assigned both a global (G) and state (S) rank on a scale of 1 to 5. Global ranks are assigned through a collaborative process involving both NatureServe and individual Natural Heritage Program scientists. State ranks are assigned by scientists within the Natural Heritage Program with the proviso that state rank cannot be rarer than indicated by the global rank.

A rank of G1 indicates critical imperilment on a global basis; the species is at great risk of extinction. S1 indicates critical imperilment within a particular state, regardless of its status elsewhere. A number of factors, such as the total range, the number of occurrences, severity of threats, and resilience contribute to the assignment of global and state ranks. The information supporting these ranks is developed and maintained by the Natural Heritage Program and NatureServe. Only state ranks are present in the association descriptions. Global rank is available on NatureServe explorer for the associations which have been assigned a NatureServe Code.

Uncertainty in conservation rank is expressed as a Range Rank. For example, S2S3 indicates a range of uncertainty such that there is a roughly equal chance of S2 or S3 and other ranks are less likely. A rank of SU expresses that a rank is unable to be assigned to an association due to lack of information or due to conflicting information about status or trends. When the taxonomic distinctiveness of an association is questionable, it is assigned a rank of SQ in combination with a standard numerical S rank, for example S3Q

Ranking for this project considered any previous ranking effort for the association or synonym listed by NatureServe, WNHP or adjacent heritage programs. In estimating the primary rank factor, the number of plots number was used as surrogate for abundance of an association within parks and throughout the state. Observational experience of land-use patterns influencing or threatening the abundance or ecological integrity of associations on and off NPS land was a secondary factor used in estimating ranks.

State Rank definitions:

  S1 critically imperiled
  S2 imperiled
  S3 vulnerable to extirpation or extinction
  S4 apparently secure
  S5 demonstrably widespread, abundant, and secure

Taxonomic Treatments

The primary source of species identification regionally is Hitchcock and Cronquist (1973) although NPS crews used more recent treatments for some species. The standard for the NatureServe IVC/NVC plant association names is Kartesz, J.T. (1999). The 2008 FGDC states: "Nomenclature for vascular plant taxa used in scientific type names should follow the accepted name in USDA PLANTS or ITIS..." with reference to version. For this report, species are synonomized according to Kartesz (2004) and are used in the tables and type descriptions. When the Kartesz (2004) name differs from Hitchcock and Cronquist (1973) in association descriptions, the latter appears in parenthesis preceded with an "=", for example, *Maianthemum (=Smilacina) stellatum* and *Agrostis pallens (=diegoensis)*.

Certain species groups warrant special discussion either from identification difficulties or non-subspecific identification needed to synonomize entities to the current nomenclatural standard. Following NatureServe nomenclatural protocol, when taxa are considered equivalent indicators and/or their field identification easily confused, the entities are included in parenthesis. For example, *Achlys triphylla* and *Achlys californica* are combined and listed as *Achlys (californica, triphylla)*.

Agrostis diegoensis - A. pallens

Kartesz (2004) and ITIS (Aug. 2008) synonomize *Agrostis diegoensis* Vasey under *A. pallens* Trin. Hitchcock and Cronquist (1973), Buckingham and others (1995) and Beik (2000) recognize the former as a dry site species found from sea level to upper treeline and the latter as a coastal sand dune species. This report lists this species as *Agrostis pallens*.

Achlys triphylla - A. californica

Kartesz (2004) and ITIS (Aug. 2008) recognize *Achlys triphylla* (Sm.) DC and *Achlys californica* I. Fukuda & H.G. Baker in Washington while Hitchcock and Cronquist (1973) recognize only the former. Buckingham and others (1995) state that *A. californica* is the common species in forests of the Olympic Peninsula and that *A. triphylla* is only mid-montane to subalpine and mostly in more open habitats. Chappell concludes from field experience that *A. californica* is the exclusive taxon in western Washington. All legacy data (399 plots) lists only *A. triphylla*. Recent NPS plot data lists *A. californica* primarily in OLYM (42 plots) with two plots in MORA. Recent plot data lists 109 MORA plots and 32 OLYM plots as *A. triphylla*. Because legacy data does not distingush *Achlys triphylla* and *Achlys californica*, they are combined and listed as *Achlys (californica, triphylla)*.

Caltha biflora – Caltha leptosepala

Caltha leptosepala is listed in 44 plots (38 legacy), *C. biflora* in 28 legacy plots and *C. leptosepala* ssp. *howellii* 6 plots. Hitchcock and Cronquist (1973) recognize two species of *Caltha*: *C. bifolia* DC. (var. *rotundifolia* (Huth) Hitchc.) and *C. leptosepala* DC. (var. sulfurea Hitchc.). Kartesz (2004) and ITIS (Aug. 2008) list *C. biflora* under *C. leptosepala* ssp. *howellii* and *C. biflora* var. *rotundifolia* under *C. leptosepala* var. *leptosepala*. Buckingham and others (1995) in the Olympics and Biek (2000) at Mount Rainier list both subspecies of *C. leptosepala*. The Flora of North America recognizes only *C. leptosepala* and no subspecies. For this project, the subspecies are combined and appear as *Caltha leptosepala (=biflora, leptosepala)*.

Festuca ovina

Festuca ovina is listed in 125 legacy plots (27 MORA, 96 OLYM, 2 other), *Festuca saximontana* appears in 1 OLYM plot, and *F. brachyphylla* in 1 NOCA and 5 MORA plots. *Festuca ovina* L. is not native to the Pacific Northwest, Hitchcock and Cronquist (1973) recognized two native varieties: *Festuca ovina* L. var. *brevifolia* (R. Br.) Wats. and *Festuca ovina* L. var. *rydbergii* St.-Yves. Kartesz (2004) and ITIS (Aug. 2008) list the former under *Festuca brachyphylla* Schult. ex Schult. & Schult. ssp. *brachyphylla* and the latter as *Festuca saximontana* Rydb. var. *saximontana*. Buckingham and others (1995) lists *F. saximontana* in alpine habitats on the Olympic Peninsula. Biek (2000) lists *F. brachyphylla* at Mount Rainier. For this project, *Festuca brachyphylla* and *F. saximontana* are combined in the synthesis tables as *Festuca (brachyphylla, saximontana)* and Olympic data is assumed to be *F. saximontana* and Cascades data to be *F. brachyphylla* and discussed as such in the type descriptions.

Lupinus latifolius – Lupinus arcticus ssp. subalpinus

Lupinus arcticus ssp. *subalpinus* appears in 101 plots, *Lupinus latifolius* ssp. *latifolius* in 51 plots and *Lupinus latifolius* without subspecies in 671 legacy plots. Hitchcock and Cronquist (1973) recognized two varieties of *Lupinus latifolius* Agardh: *subalpinus* (Piper & B.L. Rob.) and *latifolius*. Kartesz (2004) and ITIS (Aug. 2008) lists the former as a synonym of *Lupinus arcticus* S. Watson ssp. *subalpinus* (Piper & B.L. Rob.) D. Dunn and the latter as a synonym of *Lupinus latifolius* Lindl. ex J. Agardh ssp. *latifolius*. Buckingham and others (1995) describe the habitat of *L. latifolius* as "open" and *L. arcticus* as "scree" and both occurring at subalpine elevations. Biek (2000) at Mount Rainier notes that *L. latifolius* is common below 5000 feet in forest openings and that *L. arcticus* is the dominant subalpine meadow lupine species. Plots with a subspecies determination do not clearly segregate by habitat. Additionally, field crews found species identification difficult. As a result, *Lupinus arcticus* ssp. *subalpinus* and *Lupinus latifolius* ssp. *latifolius* are combined and listed as *Lupinus (arcticus ssp. subalpinus, latifolius)*.

Lupinus lepidus – Lupinus sellulus

Lupinus lepidus appears in 63 plots (61 legacy) and *Lupinus sellulus* Kellogg var. *lobbii* in 50 plots (47 legacy). Hitchcock and Cronquist (1973) recognized five varieties of *Lupinus lepidus* Dougl. including var. *lobbii* (Gray) Hitchc. Kartesz (2003) and ITIS (Aug. 2008) synonomize that variety under *Lupinus sellulus* Kellogg ssp. *sellulus* var. *lobbii* (Gray ex S. Wats) Cox. Because all legacy plots are high elevation and *L. lepidus* Dougl. ex Lindel is a lowland western Washington species and the other Hitchcock and Cronquist (1973) varieties are outside of the range of the national parks surveyed, *L. lepidus* in all legacy plots are considered *Lupinus sellulus* Kellogg var. *lobbii*.

Luzula campestris

Luzula campestris (L.) DC is an uncommon introduced weed at low elevations, not typically occurring in naturally vegetated areas (Flora of North America). It is listed in 247 plots (19 NOCA, 10 MORA, 217 OLYM, 1 other), 229 of which are legacy plots all of which are assumed to be in naturally vegetated areas. According to the University of Washington Burke Museum Herbarium: "The name *Luzula campestris* has long been misapplied to several of our species of *Luzula*, including *L. comosa* and *L. multiflora*. Hitchock and Cronquist's treatment of *L. campestris* is incorrect; see Flora of North America Volume 22 for accurate treatments." Hitchcock and Cronquist (1973) recognized three varieties: *congesta* (Thuill.) Mey., *frigida*

Buch. and *multiflora* (Ehrh.) Celek. ITIS (Aug. 2008) lists all three *L. campestris* varieties as *L. campestris*. Kartesz (2004) and ITIS (Aug. 2008) list *L. campestris* var. *congesta* (Thuill.) Mey. under *L. congesta* (Thuill.) Lej. (4 plots). The Washington Flora Checklist (October 2008 http://biology.burke.washington.edu/waflora/checklist.php) and Beik (2000) consider *L. congesta* and *L. comosa* the same enitity – *L. comosa* E. Mey. This species is native to forest openings up to alpine. Kartesz (2004) and ITIS (Aug. 2008) list *L. campestris* var. *multiflora* (Ehrh.) Celak under *L. multiflora* var. *multiflora* (13 plots) which is an introduced species that grows in grasslands at low elevations. Kartesz (2004) and ITIS (Aug. 2008) synonomize *L. campestris* ssp. *frigida* Buch. under *L. multiflora* (ssp. *frigida* (Buch.) Krecz. which according to the Washington Flora Checklist (October 2008 http://biology.burke.washington.edu/waflora/checklist.php), is the introduced species *L. multiflora*. For this project, *Luzula campestris* is assumed to be *Luzula multiflora* or *L. comosa* because of its assumed native habitat and is listed as *Luzula (comosa, multiflora)* in tables and descriptions of low elevation associations. Higher elevation associations are assumed to be native vegetation and are listed as *Luzula comosa (=campestris, congesta)* in the association descriptions.

Luzula divaricata
Luzula divaricata is listed in 4 MORA plots. Kartesz (2004) does not recognize *L. divaricata* S. Wats.in Washington although ITIS (Aug. 2008) accepts that entity. According to the Washington Flora Checklist (October 2008 http://biology.burke.washington.edu/waflora/checklist.php) *Luzula divaricata*, is misapplied in Hitchcock and Cronquist (1973) and is *L. parviflora* (Ehrh.) Desv. For this project, *Luzula divaricata* is considered *L. parviflora*.

Oxalis oregana – O. trilliifolia
Kartesz (2004), ITIS (Aug. 2008), and Hitchcock and Cronquist (1973) recognize *Oxalis oregana* Nutt. and *O. trilliifolia* Hook. in Washington. Buckingham and others (1995) lists only *O. oregana* as the common species in forests of the Olympic Peninsula. Beik (2000) lists *Oxalis oregana* as common below 762 m (2500 ft) and *O. trilliifolia* less commonly and appearing to higher elevations at Mount Rainier. Plot data (159 plots) lists only *O. oregana*. NatureServe lists a plant association in Oregon and Washington (that occurs in MORA and OLYM) as *Oxalis (oregana, trilliifolia)*. That association name is retained.

Solidago spathulata
Kartesz (2004) synonomizes *Solidago spathulata* DC. (22 MORA legacy plots) under *S. simplex* Kunth and *Solidago spathulata* DC var. *nana* (Gray) Cronq.under *S. simplex* Kunth ssp. *simplex* var. *nana* (Gray) Ringus (7 MORA legacy plots). Beik (2000) only recognizes *S. simplex* Kunth ssp. *simplex* var. *nana* (Gray) Ringus at Mount Rainier. For this project, all *Solidago spathulata* is considered to be *S. simplex* var. *nana*.

Vaccinium alaskaense (V. alaskaensis)
Kartesz (1999) synonomized *Vaccinium alaskaense* and *V. ovalifolium* under *V. alaskaensis* and NatureServe retains this treatment. Kartesz (2004) recognized *V. alaskaensis* and *V. ovalifolium* as a separate species. USDA PLANTS and ITIS (Aug. 2008) list *V. alaskaense* as in Hitchcock and Cronquest (1973). This report uses *Vaccinium alaskaense* and *V. ovalifolium*.

Results

Plant Association Descriptions

Final descriptions represent how plant associations appear, on average, at MORA, NOCA and OLYM (Appendix A). The descriptions are based on summarized plot data and existing literature. A total of 311 upland and forested wetland types are described. Over half (188) of the described associations are tree-dominated, 53 are shrub-dominated, 43 are herbaceous-dominated and 27 are sparse or lithomorphic vegetation types. Of those associations, 49 may occur in the parks based on description from literature in adjacent areas but are not represented by current plot data from within park boundaries.

Most of the described associations (153) are represented by data collected in five or more plots from MORA, NOCA and/or OLYM. Table 2 summarizes the number of plots which support plant associations, organized by life form categories. Fourteen variants of associations (20 plots) are discussed within the context of one of the described associations but appear separately in the synthesis tables (Appendix C). Global (rangewide) descriptions are not included in this report. A limited set of global association descriptions are available on NatureServe explorer.

Table 2. Numbers of plant associations within plot number and life-form categories at MORA, NOCA and OLYM.

Life form Category	Number of Plots				Total Associations
	0	1	2 - 4	5 +	
Tree	39	27	37	85	**188**
Shrub	5	10	12	26	**53**
Herbaceous	4	5	9	25	**43**
Sparse	1	3	8	15	**27**
Total Associations	**49**	**44**	**66**	**153**	**311**

Each description includes scientific name, common name, a NatureServe Code when present, acronym (that cross-references to synthesis tables), national vegetation hierarchy levels including alliance, classification confidence, range in Washington, environmental features, USFWS wetland classification, vegetation description, state conservation rank, rank justification, comments, and plant association synonyms in previous classifications.

A field key to plant association identification preceeds the association descriptions, in Appendix A. Supporting synthesis tables of these associations are organized in Appendix C. The synthesis table lists a subset of species found in each association, with constancy and average cover values. Appendix D presents a summary of a selected set of environmental characteristics sampled for each association at MORA, NOCA, and OLYM.

Appendix B provides 50 additional shrub and herbaceous wetland associations compiled from NatureServe, WNHP classification, literature and field experience that occur or can possibly occur in the parks. Over half (38) of those associations are supported in the current plot data. Appendix B provides the list of those wetland associations in preliminary field key format. Each wetland association includes scientific name, common name, NatureServe Code, acronym (that cross-references to synthesis tables), range in Washington, and environmental features. Larger-scale tree and shrub-dominated wetlands (7 tree-dominated and 2 shrub-dominated associations) and riparian vegetation (18 tree-dominated and 9 shrub-dominated associations) are described and represent by plot data in Appendix E. An additional four wetland and eight riparian tree-dominated associations are described from literature without plot representation but likely to occur in the parks. Fifty herbaceous wetland associations that probably occur in the parks are provided, twenty-two of which have at least one representative plot.

The 2005 preliminary classification, based on literature and existing knowledge, identified 195 probable associations: 142 tree-dominated, 25 shrub-dominated, 23 herbaceous-dominated, and 5 sparse vegetation types. Forty-four of those preliminary associations were then not supported by plot data from the parks, 141 were represented by plot data from the parks, and ten were considered variants of associations and were merged or split into other types.

The final classification step added an additional 126 associations. 54 tree-dominated, 28 shrub-dominated, 22 herbaceous-dominated, and 22 sparse vegetation types. Five of those additional associations are not currently supported by plot data but are described in literature as on or near MORA, NOCA, or OLYM. Fourteen of the added associations are recognized in the current NVC or are included in the coastal correlation (Meidinger 2005). Twenty are related to current NVC associations and, if not accepted as new associations, would expand the geographic range or floristic variation of the current NVC association. Eighteen are new association concepts with support in the classification literature and 40 represent entirely new association concepts generated by sampling in the parks. The remaining additional associations are provisionally recognized and most are represented by a single plot. They fall within the following general categories: avalanche tracks, lahar or debris surfaces or riparian flood terraces (22) or are map assessment plots (7) that could either represent more widespread types or prove to be outliers during subsequent mapping efforts.

An evaluation of the number of plots per park may be used to assess the relative coverage of the classification sampling effort. OLYM has the most plots-1661, followed by MORA- 931 plots and NOCA- 272. The latter two parks are augmented by 270 plots from within approximately 10 miles of their eastern boundaries. Forests are the dominant physiognomic class on all parks and the plot distribution reflects that characteristic. OLYM has the widest representation of physiognomic categories among the parks (Table 3). Sparse vegetation sampling is least represented at NOCA. That vegetation type is classified primarily from plots on OLYM and is probably the least represented category in this classification.

Table 3. The distribution of final plots expressed as percent by physiognomic category among MORA, NOCA, and OLYM.

Lifeform Category	Percentage of Plots				
	MORA	**NOCA**	**OLYM**	**Other**	**All Parks**
Tree	72.4%	64.7%	37.4%	41.5%	**50.7%**
Shrub	14.7%	23.5%	18.6%	20.7%	**18.1%**
Herbaceous	10.4%	11.4%	26.1%	33.7%	**20.9%**
Sparse	2.5%	0.4%	17.9%	4.1%	**10.7%**
Total Plots	**931**	**272**	**1661**	**270**	**3134**

Legacy plots represent over half of the plots used in classification, with most of those from OLYM. NOCA has no legacy plots (Table 4). In addition, OLYM has the greatest number and NOCA the least of the NPS crew plots. In spite of the lowest overall sampling, NOCA has the highest percentage of NPS herbaceous plots.

Table 4. The distribution of legacy and NPS plots expressed as percent by physiognomic category among MORA, NOCA, and OLYM.

Lifeform Category	Percentage of Legacy Plots			
	MORA	**OLYM**	**Other**	**All Parks**
Tree	76.0%	27.4%	41.5%	**42.7%**
Shrub	8.5%	19.2%	20.7%	**16.4%**
Herbaceous	12.7%	31.1%	33.7%	**26.3%**
Sparse	2.7%	22.3%	4.1%	**14.6%**
Total Plots	**622**	**1338**	**270**	**2230**

Lifeform Category	Percentage of NPS Plots			
	MORA	**NOCA**	**OLYM**	**All Parks**
Tree	65.0%	64.7%	78.6%	**69.8%**
Shrub	27.2%	23.5%	16.1%	**22.1%**
Herbaceous	5.8%	11.4%	5.3%	**7.3%**
Sparse	1.9%	0.4%	0.0%	**0.8%**
Total Plots	**309**	**272**	**323**	**904**

Association Results

The most sampled plant associations by physiognomic group give an indication (sampling is not random) of their relative abundance within the parks. The most sampled forest associations are subalpine types: *Tsuga mertensiana-Abies amabilis/Rhododendron albiflorum* Forest (66 plots),

Abies lasiocarpa-(Abies amabilis)/Vaccinium membranaceum/Valeriana sitchensis Forest (52 plots), and upper montane types *Tsuga heterophylla-Abies amabilis/Vaccinium alaskaense/Rubus pedatus* Forest (45 plots), *Abies amabilis/Vaccinium membranaceum /Rubus lasiococcus* Forest (44 plots), and *Tsuga heterophylla-Abies amabilis-(Pseudotsuga menziesii)/Vaccinium alaskaense* Forest (41 plots).

The most sampled shrub associations are alpine and subalpine dwarf-shrub types: *Phyllodoce empetriformis-Vaccinium deliciosum-(Cassiope mertensiana)* Subalpine Dwarf-shrubland (102 plots), *Cassiope mertensiana-Phyllodoce empetriformis* Alpine Dwarf-shrubland (65 plots), and *Vaccinium deliciosum* Dwarf-shrubland (52 plots), *Juniperus communis-(Phlox diffusa)* Dwarf-shrubland (40 plots), and the avalanche/riparian-associated tall shrubland *Alnus viridis ssp. sinuata-Rubus spectabilis/Athyrium filix-femina* Shrubland (27 plots).

The most sampled herbaceous associations are high elevation mesic grassland and forb meadows: *Luetkea pectinata* Herbaceous Vegetation (71 plots), *Carex spectabilis-(Lupinus (arcticus, latifolius)-Polygonum bistortoides* Herbaceous Vegetation (64 plots), *Phlox diffusa-(Lomatium martindalei-Carex phaeocephala)* Herbaceous Vegetation (55 plots), and *Lupinus (arcticus ssp. subalpinus, latifolius)* Herbaceous Vegetation (47 plots) and alpine/subalpine grassland *Festuca roemeri-(Phlox diffusa-Arenaria capillaris)* Herbaceous Vegetation (52 plots). These summaries are mostly legacy plots.

The most sampled sparse association are *Astragalus cottonii* Lithomorphic Vegetation (48 plots), *Phlox diffusa* Lithomorphic Vegetation (34 plots), *Juniperus communis* Lithomorphic Vegetation (25 plots), *Phacelia hastata* Lithomorphic Vegetation (24 plots), and *Delphinium glareosum* Lithomorphic Vegetation (23 plots). These are mostly OLYM legacy plots.

Preliminary associations represent new associations to the NVC. Over half of the preliminary forest associations are supported by descriptions in the literature. Those forest associations without supporting literature appear in two general categories: 1) new classification units representing existing vegetation that were only implicitly recognized in previous Pacific Northwest forest association classifications that emphasized late seral vegetation. An example is the *Pseudotsuga menziesii/Achlys triphylla* Forest, and 2) associations with affinities to complex classification units found east of the Cascade crest in Washington and British Columbia, for example *Abies lasiocarpa-Pseudotsuga menziesii/Mahonia nervosa* Forest. Most preliminary sparse vegetation types represent new vegetation classification units that were underrepresented or not sampled in previous classification work in the region.

Imperiled Associations

The classification includes seven associations ranked S1 (indicating critical imperilment within the state of Washington), eighteen ranked S2 (imperiled) and eight associations have a range rank of S1S2 (critically imperiled or imperiled). Ranks of S1 to S2 are an estimate of rarity based on restricted or unique habitat and/or threatened habitats. Six of the S1 associations occur in restricted habitats although three coastal forest associations (*Picea sitchensis/Maianthemum dilatatum, Picea sitchensis/Vaccinium ovatum*, and *Tsuga heterophylla-Abies amabilis-(Thuja plicata)/Vaccinium alaskaense/Blechnum spicant* Forests) have been reduced in overall ecological quality by past timber harvesting on and off national park land. Three S1 grassland

associations (*Calamagrostis nutkaensis-Vicia nigra ssp. gigantea-(Equisetum telmateia),
Festuca roemeri-Cerastium arvense-Koeleria macrantha and Festuca roemeri-Plectritis
congesta* Herbaceous associations) are restricted environmentally to forest openings and are
threatened by exotic species invasion with site disturbance and tree invasion, particularly the
Festuca roemeri associations. The *Pinus ponderosa/Pseudoroegneria spicata* Woodland
association which is possible at NOCA, previously had a wider range in Washington but its
extent has been greatly reduced due to removal of larger trees, fire suppression and invasive
species.

Three S1S2 associations are occur along OLYM's narrow wilderness coast. The *Thuja plicata-
Tsuga heterophylla/Lysichiton americanus/Sphagnum spp.* Woodland is found only in coastal
bogs and fens. *Thuja plicata-Tsuga heterophylla/Vaccinium ovatum* Forest, a very late-seral
stage forest and *Tsuga heterophylla-Thuja plicata-(Abies amabilis)/Gaultheria
shallon/Blechnum spicant* Forest occur only along the coast as regionally endemic associations.
Non- protected lands supporting the latter two associations along the coast have largely been
converted or modified by logging. Two S1S2 whitebark pine communities are fairly widely
distributed but restricted to small patches in the high elevations of the eastern Cascades in
northern Washington and OLYM. The ecological condition of occurrences is declining due to
Pinus albicaulis mortality from fire exclusion and white pine blister rust (*Cronartium ribicola*).
As result, the *Pinus albicaulis/Festuca viridula* Woodland and *Pinus albicaulis-(Tsuga
mertensiana)/Luzula glabrata var. hitchcockii* Woodland associations are increasingly rare, and
are likely to continue to decline. The non-forest S1S2 associations are *Vaccinium deliciosum-
Tauschia stricklandii* Dwarf-shrubland,endemic to MORA,occurs in small patches in subalpine
settings where recreational impacts of trampling and trail proliferation pose a possible threat, and
Koeleria macrantha-(Agrostis pallens) Herbaceous Vegetation found only on balds in the
Cascades is subject to tree and exotic species invasions.

Fifteen of the eighteen S2 associations are restricted environmentally, four are wetland or
riparian forest types, five are subalpine woodlands, three are subalpine or alpine herbaceous
types, two are forest associations with east Cascade affinities and one is a grassland bald. Three
S2 associations are less restricted environmentally but have reduced occurrences due to
vegetation alteration from timber harvesting and land conversion (*Pseudotsuga
menziesii/Gaultheria shallon-Holodiscus discolor* and *Pinus contorta var. contorta-Pseudotsuga
menziesii/Gaultheria shallon* Forest associations. nly the former has been confirmed on OLYM)
One S2 association possible at NOCA (*Purshia tridentata/Pseudoroegneria spicata* Shrubland)
is subject to both land conversion and exotic species invasion.

Discussion

Contributions of This Work

Prior to this project, vegetation sampling and classification concentrated on the abundant forest landscape on and off park lands and on special environments at high elevation, primarily alpine and subalpine dwarf-shrubland and herbaceous vegetation. The targeted sampling effort has allowed some physiognomic or ecologic niches such as avalanche tracks or montane shrublands to be better understood in the region. As directed, the NPS crews accumulated 109 shrub plots that contributed to defining forty of fifty-two shrubland associations in this document. Specifically, variation within thirteen NVC (NatureServe) shrubland associations was described and verified as being on NPS land. Eleven associations that were tentatively recognized from literature and field experience were newly described and verified as occurring within the parks. Provisionally, eight new associations are described pending more survey beyond NPS land to verify the range of variation of types or their relationship to associations recognized elsewhere. These associations provide a foundation from which to more fully describe shrublands and their relationships to natural processes in the Pacific Northwest.

This project provided the opportunity to test the classification of new associations and revisions to the existing NatureServe (2005) from the coastal forests correlation project (CFCP) (Meidinger et al. 2005), since the results of that multi-jurisdictional project served as the basis for forest classification. This project confirmed eighty-seven NatureServe and forty-four CFCP associations as recognizable units and as being on NPS land. Twenty-seven new forest associations were described not previous recognized by NatureServe or the CFCP. Nine of those types represent new associations not currently recognized elsewhere. Provisionally, thirty-four new forest associations are pending more survey or analysis beyond NPS land to verify the range of variation of types or their relationship to associations recognized elsewhere.

Because most of the non-forest alpine and subalpine vegetation in the coastal Pacific Northwest occurs on MORA, NOCA and OLYM, this project provided the opportunity to evaluate its classification through comparison of both legacy data and new NPS data. This project clarified the classification and distribution of twenty-one previously recognized NVC high-elevation non-forest associations and more formally recognized nine new associations cited from literature. An additional eleven new non-forest associations were described to better characterize this high-elevation landscape. Eight provisonal associations were proposed pending more survey or analysis beyond NPS land to verify the range of variation of types or their relationship to associations recognized elsewhere.

Not only has this project filled in gaps and clarified previous classification efforts, this work greatly contributes to the regional and even national organization of vegetation information. Through cooperative project with NatureServe, the association level classification developed for these parks is being used to develop the 2008 NVC hierarchy for the region. Associations provide the reference for evaluating relationships among the various upper levels of the NVC. NatureServe collaborated with WNHP to develop the alliance-level concepts for these classifications by providing a review of the analytical results, review of the plant associations determined by WNHP and wrote descriptions for the alliances and alliance groups with input from WNHP. This work included determination of all plant associations and their relationship to alliance, group level and other higher levels of the Pacific Northwest portion of the new NVC hierarchy.

This project helps clarify the important role MORA, NOCA and OLYM play in the protection of state and globally rare vegetation. Through sampling and developing the classification, eighteen state critically imperiled or imperiled associations are recognized and confirmed on national parks. These state rare associations are **not** confined to national parks and are located in appropriate environments elsewhere in the state. The parks though support important protection of some of the least altered representatives of these types in Washington, particularly low elevation forests along the coast strip and foothills of OLYM. High elevation forest, woodlands and grasslands are well represented in all the parks and offer the most natural setting for representation of those associations in the state.

Gaps in the Classification

In contrast to using a systematic stratified, or gradient-transect sampling approach to sampling the landscape, the NPS field crews were directed to sample plots that would 1) augment the description and distribution of known associations and 2) sample vegetation not represented in the current classification, for example shrub-dominated vegetation. This approach allowed the NPS to take maximum advantage of previous regional classification work, and seemed the best viable option for 12 people to sample nearly 2 million acres during only 2 field seasons.

From a whole-park perspective, the classification for OLYM is likely the most complete based on total plots and range of physiognomic categories classified. MORA is well represented in forest classification and appears to also be well represented in shrub and herbaceous classification. In contrast, NOCA is the least sampled and contains a complex of vegetation for which the classification is most likely to need further modifications and updates during mapping.

This project's objective was to provide a vegetation classification that would support planned vegetation mapping, consequently, minimal effort went to sampling small-scale associations such as those occurring within wetland patches. Additionally, wetland vegetation is under sampled because it requires a different sampling protocol and additional training of field personnel. Although larger forested and shrub wetlands are fairly described, more the half of the wetland herb types that are likely to occur in the parks are not sampled.

Sparsely vegetated areas or lithomorphic vegetation was largely unsampled during this project and are represented mostly by legacy plots from OLYM. Sparse areas pose unique challenges for both sampling and classification analysis because of their low species diversity, importance of non-vascular species, small patch size and high landscape heterogeneity. Developing a better classification for these small-scale associations would require a higher sampling intensity than was supported. Furthermore, these associations are found in some of the most difficult terrain to access in the parks.

In addition to addressing these known gaps, further sampling may help reduce confusion between certain types. Associations identified in this project as CFCP types (Meidinger et al. 2005) that are represented by only a few plots and have distributions primarily north in BC or south in Oregon would benefit from further clarification. For example, the *Populus balsamifera ssp. trichocarpa-Alnus rubra/Carex obnupta* association as recognized in this report is the CFCP *Populus balsamifera* spp. *trichocarpa/ Cornus sericea/Carex obnupta* (PNWCOAST_113). Inclusion of these western Olympic plots with this type expanded the Puget Trough/Georgia Strait concept to include riverine associated wetlands, a much wetter climate, and differing associated species. The *Pseudotsuga menziesii-(Abies grandis)/Acer circinatum/Polystichum munitum* association is a newly recognized association in this report as a result of the coastal correlation from northwest Oregon and new in Washington. Although not represented in the current data for national parks in Washington further sampling is needed to better characterize this association in Washington.

Provisional types in this report also indicate gaps or need for addition classification attention. Many provisional units are placeholders for groups of plots that can be classified to alliance or higher hierarchical levels, such as *Ceanothus velutinus* Shrubland, *Spiraea splendens* Shrubland and *Vaccinium scoparium* Shrubland. Other provisional types defined from park plots appear to be variants of vegetation described elsewhere, for example *Cupressus nootkatensis /Vaccinium deliciosum* Provisional Forest appears to be a variant of *Tsuga mertensiana/Phyllodoce empetriformis-Vaccinium deliciosum.* The *Pseudotsuga menziesii-(Pinus ponderosa / Symphoricarpos albus* Provisional Forest is either a variant of or is the same as *Pseudotsuga menziesii/Symphoricarpos albus* Forest found in the east Cascades and Northern Rockies.

Future Directions
This report summarizes current available data and literature, and therefore represents the latest approximation of the plant associations on MORA, NOCA and OLYM. Continuation of this project into a vegetation mapping phase undoubtedly will reveal associations not covered in the current classification or will add to the variation described by it. The WNHP coordinates with NatureServe to maintain and update the NVC and will continue in that role during the mapping phases of the project. A final approximation of the plant associations of MORA, NOCA and OLYM will incorporate new sampling and any updates to this classification will be incorporated into the NVC.

Conclusions

The project met its goal of developing a single vegetation classification of plant associations for MORA, NOCA and OLYM. The plant associations described in Appendix A reflect the most current and comprehensive vegetation classification not only for the parks, but for the region. This work also represents a philosophical shift in this region from describing and mapping vegetation based on potential vegetation relative to bioclimatic zones to one that is based on existing vegetation. The field keys and descriptions which comprise this report will provide NPS staff, natural resource managers from other agencies, and researchers the tools necessary to sample vegetation in a manner that will closely tie their work to the forthcoming NPS vegetation maps. The combined NCCN classification and mapping work not only provides park managers information for land use decisions, but also informs park visitors, guides research and will serve as a baseline against which to evaluate future vegetation change.

Literature Cited

Agee, J. K. and J. Kertis. 1987. Forest types of the North Cascades National Park Service Complex. Can. J. Botany **65**: 1520:1530.

Almack, J.A., W.L. Gaines, R.H. Naney, P.H. Morrison, J.R. Eby, G.F. Wooten, M.C. Snyder, S.H. Fitkin, E.R. Garcia. 1993. North Cascades Grizzly Bear Ecosystem Evaluation. Report to the Interagency Grizzly Bear Committee in fulfillment of requirements identified in the 1982 Grizzly Bear Recovery Plan.

Alt, D. and D. W. Hyndman. 2001. Northwest Exposures. A Geologic Story of the Northwest. Mountain Press Publishing Company. Missoula, MT.

Alverson, E. and J. Arnett. 1986. From the steppe to the alpine: a botanical reconnaissance of the Lake Chelan-Sawtooth Ridge Area, Washington. *In* Plant of Life of the North Cascades: Lake Chelan-Sawtooth Ridge, Stehekin Valley, and Glacier Peak. Douglasia Occasional Papers. Washington Native Plant Society. Vol. 2.

Apostol, D. and M. Sinclair. 2006. Restoring the Pacific Northwest. The Art and Science of Ecological Restoration in Cascadia. Island Press. Washington D.C.

Arno, S.F. and R. P. Hammerly. 2007. Northwest Trees. Identifying and Understanding the Region's Native Trees. The Mountaineers Books. Seattle, WA.

Belsky, J., and R. del Moral. 1982. Ecology of an alpine-subalpine meadow complex in the Olympic Mountains, Washington. Can. J. Botany **60**: 779-788.

Biek, D. 2000. Flora of Mount Rainier National Park. Oregon State University Press. Corvallis, OR.

Bigley, R. and S. Hull. 1995. Draft Guide to Plant Associations on the Olympic Experimental Forest. Washington Dept. Natural Resources, Olympia, WA.

Brubaker, L.B. 1991. Climate Change and the Origin of Old-Growth Douglas-Fir Forests in the Puget Sound Lowland. *In* Wildlife and Vegetation of Douglas-Fir Unmanaged Forests. Ruggiero, L. F.; K.B. Aubry; B. Carey; M.H. Huff (tech. eds). General Technical Report PNW-GTR-285. U.S. Forest Service, Portland, Oregon.

Buckingham, N.M., E.G. Schreiner, T.N. Kaye, J.E. Burger, and E.L. Tisch. 1995. Flora of the Olympic Peninsula. Northwest Interpretive Association and Washington Native Plant Society. Seattle, WA.

Burtchard, G.C. 1998. Environment, Prehistory & Archaeology of Mount Rainier National Park, Washington. International Archaeological Research Institute, Inc. Prepared for National Park Service, Seattle, Washington. Online.
http://www.nps.gov/archive/mora/ncrd/archaeology/index.htm

Burtchard, G.C., B. Diaz, and KI. Carlisle. 2008. Paradise Camp. Archaeology in the Paradise Developed Area, Mount Rainier National Park. National Park Service, Seattle, WA. Online. http://www.nps.gov/mora/historyculture/upload/Paradise%20Camp%20Report%20for%20Adobe%20Reader.pdf

Catton. T. 1996. Wonderland: An Administrative History of Mount Rainier National Park. National Park Service, Seattle, WA. Online. http://www.nps.gov/mora/historyculture/administrative-history.htm

Chappell, C.B. 1999. Ecological Classification of Low-elevation Riparian Vegetation on the Olympic Experimental State Forest: A First Approximation (DRAFT). Washington Department of Natural Resources, Natural Heritage Program. Olympia, WA.

Chappell, C.B., R.C. Crawford, C. Barrett, J. Kagan, D.H. Johnson, M. O'Mealy, G.A. Green, H.L. Ferguson, W.D. Edge, E.L. Greda, and T.A. O'Neil. 2001. Wildlife habitats: descriptions, status, trends, and system dynamics. Pages 22-114 in Johnson, D.H., and T.A. O'Neil, dirs. Wildlife-Habitat Relationships in Oregon and Washington. Oregon State Univ. Press, Corvallis, OR.

Chappell, C.B. 2006. Plant Associations of Balds and Bluffs of Western Washington. Washington Department of Natural Resources, Natural Heritage Program. Olympia, WA. Online at: http://www1.dnr.wa.gov/nhp/refdesk/communities/pdf/balds_veg.pdf

Climate Impact Group. 2008. About Pacific Northwest Climate. Online. http://cses.washington.edu/cig/pnwc/pnwc.shtml

Cushman, M.J. 1981. The influence of recurrent snow avalanches on vegetation patterns in the Washington Cascades. Dissertation. University of Washington, Seattle, WA.

Dale, V.D., F.J. Swanson and C. M. Crisafulli. 2005. Ecological Responses to the 1980 Eruption of Mount St. Helens. New York, NY, Springer.

del Moral, R., A. F. Watson, and R. S. Fleming. 1976. Vegetation structure in the Alpine Lakes region of Washington State: classification of vegetation on granitic rocks. Syesis: 291-316.

del Moral, R. and J.N. Long. 1977. Classification of montane forest community types in the Cedar River drainage of western Washington, U.S.A. Can. J. For. Res. 7(2):217-225.

Douglas, G.W. 1969. A Preliminary Biological Survey of the North Cascades National Park and the Ross Lake and Lake Chelan National Recreation Areas. National Park Service. Sedro Woolley, WA.

Douglas, G.W. 1971. An ecological survey of potential natural areas in the North Cascades National Park complex. Unpublished Report. State of Washington Intercampus Education and Scientific Preserves Committee.

Douglas, G. W. 1972. Subalpine plant communities of the western North Cascades, Washington. Arctic and Alpine Research **4**: 147-166.

Douglas, G. W., and L. C. Bliss. 1977. Alpine and high subalpine plant communities of the North Cascades Range, Washington and British Columbia. Ecol. Monographs **47**: 113-150.

Dunwiddie, P.W. 1983. Holocene forest dynamics on Mount Rainier, Washington. Dissertation. University of Washington, Seattle, WA.

Driscoll, R.E. et al. 1984. An ecological land classification framework for the United States. USDA Forest Service, Misc. Pub. 1439. Washington, DC: U.S. Department of Agriculture, Forest Service.

Edwards, O.M. 1980. The alpine vegetation of Mount Rainier National Park: Structure, constraints, and development. Dissertation. University of Washington, Seattle, WA.

Federal Geographic Data Committee. 1997. National Vegetation Classification Standard, FGDC-STD-005. Vegetation Subcommittee, Federal Geographic Data Committee. FGDC Secretariat, U.S. Geological Survey. Reston, VA.

Federal Geographic Data Committee. 2008. National Vegetation Classification Standard, Version 2. FGDC-STD-005-2008. Vegetation Subcommittee, Federal Geographic Data Committee. FGDC Secretariat, U.S. Geological Survey. Reston, VA. Online. http://www.fgdc.gov/standards/projects/FGDC-standards-projects/vegetation/NVCS V2_FINAL_2008-02.pdf

Flinn, K.M., M.J. Lechowicz, and M.J. Waterway. 2008. Plant species diversity and composition of wetlands within an upland forest. American Journal of Botany Vol. **95**: 1216-1224.

Flahault, C., and C. Schroter. 1910. Rapport sur la nomenclature phytogeopraphique. Proceedings of the Third International Botanical Congress, Brussels 1:131-164.

Fonda, R.W. 1974. Forest succession in relation to river terrace development in Olympic National Park, Washington. Ecology **55**:927-942.

Fonda, R.W., and L.C. Bliss. 1969. Forest Vegetation of Montane and subalpine zones, Olympic Mountains, Washington. Ecol. Mono. **39**:271-301.

Franklin, J.F. and C.T. Dyrness. 1988. Natural Vegetation of Oregon and Washington. Oregon State University Press. Corvallis, OR.

Franklin, J.F. and J.M. Trapper. 1963. Plant communities of the northern Cascade Range: a reconnaissance. Northwest Science 37(4): 163-164.

Franklin, J.F., W.H. Moir, M.A. Hemstrom, S.E. Greene, and B.G. Smith. 1988. The Forest Communities of Mount Rainier National Park. Scientific Monograph Series No. 19. U.S. Department of Interior, National Park Service. Washington D.C.

Frehner, H.K. 1957. Development of soil and vegetation on the Kautz Creek flood deposit in Mount Rainier National Park. M.F. Thesis, University of Washington, Seattle, WA. 83 p.

Gavin, D.G. & L. Brubaker. 1999. A 6000-Year Soil Pollen Record of Subalpine Meadow Vegetation in the Olympic Mountains, Washington, USA. Journal of Ecology. 87(1): 106-122

Gavin, D.G., L.B. Brubaker, J.S. McLachlan, and W.W. Oswald 2005. Correspondence of pollen assemblages with forest zones across steep environmental gradients, Olympic Peninsula, Washington, USA. The Holocene 15:648-662.

Grossman D.H., Faber-Langendoen D., Weakley A.S., Anderson M., Bourgeron P., Crawford R., Goodin K., Landaal S., Metzler K., Patterson K.D., Pyne M., Reid M., and Sneddon L. 1998. International classification of ecological communities: terrestrial vegetation of the United States. Volume I, The National Vegetation Classification System: development, status, and applications. The Nature Conservancy: Arlington, VA.

Hamann, M.J. 1972. Vegetation of alpine and subalpine meadows of Mount Rainier National Park, Washington. M.S. thesis, Wash. St. Univ., Pullman.

Hemstrom, M. A., and J. F. Franklin. 1982. Fire and other disturbances of the forests in Mount Rainier National Park. Quaternary Res. **18**: 32-51.

Henderson, J.A. 1974. Composition, distribution, and succession of subalpine meadows in Mount Rainier National Park, Washington. Dissertation. Oregon State University, Corvallis, OR.

Henderson, J.A., D.H. Peter, R.D. Lesher, and D.C. Shaw. 1989. Forested Plant Associations of the Olympic National Forest. United States Department of Agriculture, Forest Service, Pacific Northwest Region. R6 ECOL Technical Paper 001-88.

Henderson, J.A., D.A. Peter, and R. Lesher. 1992. Field Guide to the Forested Plant Associations of the Mt. Baker-Snoqualmie National Forest. USDA USFS PNW Region. R6 ECOL Tech Paper 028-91.

Henderson, J.A. and R. Lesher. 2003 Survey protocols for benchmark plots (permanent intensive ecoplots) for Western Washington. Version 2.0 Western Washington Ecology Program, USDA Forest Service, Region 6.

Hitchcock, L.C. and A.Cronquest. 1973. Flora of the Pacific Northwest. Univ. Washington Press. Seattle.

Iachetti, P., J.Floberg, G. Wilhere, K. Ciruna, D. Markovic, J. Lewis, M. Heiner, G. Kittel, R. Crawford, S. Farone, S. Ford, M. Goering, D. Nicolson, S. Tyler, and P. Skidmore. 2006. North Cascades and Pacific Ranges Ecoregional Assessment, Volume 1- Report. Prepared by the Nature Conservancy of Canada, The Nature Conservancy of Washington, and the Washington Department of Fish and Wildlife with support from the British Columbia Conservation Data Centre, Washington Department of Natural Resources Natural Heritage Program, and NatureServe. Nature Conservancy of Canada, Victoria, BC.

Jennings, M.D., D. O.L. Loucks, D.C. Glenn-Lewin, R.K. Peet, Faber-Langendoen, D.H. Grossman, A. Damman, M.G. Barbour, R. Pfister, M. Walker, S.S. Talbot, J. Walker, G.S, Hartshorn, G. Waggoner, M.D. Abrams, A. Hill, M. Rejmanek, D. Roberts, and D. Tart. 2002. Standards for Associations and Alliances of the U.S. National Vegetation Classification, Version 1.0. Ecological Society of America, Vegetation Classification Panel. Washington DC.

Jennings, M.D., D. Faber-Langendoen, R.K. Peet, O.L. Loucks, D.C. Glenn-Lewin, A. Damman, M.G. Barbour, R. Pfister, D.H. Grossman, D. Roberts, D. Tart, M. Walker, S.S. Talbot, J. Walker, G.S, Hartshorn, G. Waggoner, M.D. Abrams, , A. Hill, M. Rejmanek. 2006. Description, documentation, and evaluation of associations and aAlliances within the U.S. National Vegetation Classification, Version 4.5. Ecological Society of America, Vegetation Classification Panel. Washington DC.

Jenny, H. 1941. Factors of Soil Formation. McGraw-Hill. New York, NY.

Kartesz, J.T. 1999. A synonymized checklist and atlas with biological attributes for the vascular flora of the United States, Canada, and Greenland. First edition. In: Kartesz, J.T. and C.A. Meacham. Synthesis of the North American flora [computer program]. Version 1.0. North Carolina Botanical Garden: Chapel Hill, NC

Kartesz, J.T. 2004. A synonymized checklist and atlas with biological attributes for the vascular flora of the United States, Canada, and Greenland. Second edition. In: Kartesz, J.T. and C.A. Meacham. Synthesis of the North American flora. Version 2.0. North Carolina Botanical Garden: Chapel Hill, NC

Kratz, A. M. 1975. Vegetational analysis of the coastal *Picea sitchensis* forest zone in Olympic National Park, Washington. Thesis. Western Washington State College, Bellingham, WA.

Kulzer, L. S. Luchessa, S. Cooke, R. Errington, and F. Weinmann. 2001. Characteristics of the low-elevation *Sphagnum*-dominated peatlands of western Washington: A Community Profile. Part 1: Physical, Chemical, and Vegetation Characteristics. Report prepared for U.S. Environmental Protection Agency, Region 10. Seattle, WA. Online. http://www.kingcounty.gov/environment/waterandland/stormwater/documents/sphagnum-bogs.aspx

Kuramoto, R.T. and L.C. Bliss. 1970. Ecology of Subalpine Meadows in the Olympic Mountains, Washington. Ecological Monographs **40 (3):** 314-347.

Lillybridge, T.R., B.L. Kovalchik, C.K. Williams, and B.G. Smith. 1995. Field Guide for Forested plant association of the Wenatchee National Forest. Gen Tech Rep PNW-GTR-359. U.S. Forest Service, Portland, Oregon.

McNulty, T. 2003. Olympic National Park. A Natural History. University of Washington Press. Seattle, WA.

MacKenzie, W. H. and R. Klassen. 1999. User guide for 197 ver. 2.0.Online. www.for.gov.bc.ca/research/becweb/subsitevpro/index.htm.

Meidinger, D, C. Chappell, C. Cadrin, G. Kittel, C. McCain, K. Boggs, J. Kagan, G. Cushon, A. Banner and T. DeMeo. 2005. International Vegetation Classification of the Pacific Northwest: International correlation of temperate coastal forest plant associations of Oregon, Washington, British Columbia and Alaska. Contributors: B.C. Ministry of Forests, USDA Forest Service, B.C. Conservation Data Centre, Alaska Natural Heritage Program, Washington Natural Heritage Program, Oregon Natural Heritage Information Center.

Miller, J.W. and M.M. Miller. 1970. Phytosociological reconnaissance of western redcedar stands in four valleys of the North Cascades National Park Complex. Unpublished report submitted to the National Park Service.

National Oceanic and Atmospheric Administration (NOAA). 2008. National Climatic Data Center. Online. http://www.ncdc.noaa.gov/oa/climate/extremes/1999/may/extremes0599.html. (Accessed October, 2008).

National Park Service (NPS). 2005. Mount Rainier National Park Geologic Resource Evaluation Report. Geologic Resources Division, National Park Service, U.S. Department of Interior. NPS D-535. Denver, CO. Online. http://www.nature.nps.gov/geology/inventory/publications/reports/mora_gre_rpt_view.pdf

National Park Service (NPS). 2008a. Mount Rainier National Park website. Online. http://www.nps.gov/mora/

National Park Service (NPS). 2008b. North Cascades National Park Complex website. Online. http://www.nps.gov/noca/

National Park Service (NPS). 2008c. Olympic National Park website. Online. http://www.nps.gov/olym/

NatureServe. 2005. NatureServe explorer. Online. (http://www.natureserve.org/explorer/)

Pringle, P. T. 2008. Roadside geology of Mount Rainier National Park and vicinity: Washington Division of Geology and Earth Resources Information Circular 107.

Rochefort, R.M. and D.L. Peterson. 1996. Temporal and Spatial Distribution of Trees in Subalpine Meadows of Mount Rainier National Park, Washington, U.S.A. Arctic and AlpineResearch 28(1):52-59.

Risvold, A. M., and R. W. Fonda. 2001. Community composition and floristic relationships in montane wetlands in the North Cascades, Washington. Northwest Science **75**:157-167.

Rust, S.K. 1992. Plant ecology of a coastal headland, Iceberg Point, Lopez Island, Washington. Thesis. University of Washington, Seattle, WA.

Soil Conservation Service. 1994. Keys to Soil Taxonomy. Sixth Edition. Soil Survey Staff, U.S. Department of Agriculture. Pocahontas Pres, Inc. Blacksburg, VA.

Tabor, R.W. and Haugerud, R. 1999. Geology of the North Cascades. Mountaineers. Seattle, WA.

Taylor, R.J. and G.W. Douglas. 1977. Plant Ecology and Natural History of Chowder Ridge, Mt. Baker: A Potential Alpine Research Natural Area in the Western North Cascades. Northwest Sci. **52**(1): 35-50.

UNESCO. 1973. International classification and mapping of vegetation. Series 6. Ecology and conservation. United Nations Educational, Scientific and Cultural Organization, Paris, France.

United Nations Environment Programme (UNEP). 2008. World Conservation Monitoring Centre. Online. http://www.unep-wcmc.org/sites/wh/olympic.html

Van Dyke, F. 2008. Conservation Biology: Foundations, Concepts, and Applications. 2nd Edition. Springer. New York, NY.

Washington Department of Natural Resources (WADNR). 2007. State of Washington Natural Heritage Program Plan 2007; Natural Heritage Program, Washington Department of Natural Resources. Olympia, WA.

Washington Department of Natural Resources (WADNR). 2008. Geology of Washington. Geology and Earth Resources Division, Washington Department of Natural Resources. Olympia, WA. Online: http://www.dnr.wa.gov/ResearchScience/Topics/GeologyofWashington/Pages/geolofwa.aspx

Washington Flora Checklist. October 2008. Online. http://biology.burke.washington.edu/waflora/checklist.php.

Whitlock, C. 1992. Vegetational and climatic history of the Pacific Northwest during the last 20,000 Years: Implications for understanding present-day biodiversity. The Northwest Environmental Journal 8: 5-28.

Williams, H. 2002. The Restless Northwest. A Geological Story. Washington State University Press. Pullman, WA.

NPS D-586, April 2009